Robert Florey's
Frankenstein
Starring
Bela Lugosi

Books by
Philip J Riley

CLASSIC HORROR FILMS
Frankenstein, the original 1931 shooting script
Bride of Frankenstein, the original 1935 shooting script
Son of Frankenstein, the original 1939 shooting script
Ghost of Frankenstein, the original 1942 shooting script
Frankenstein Meets the Wolfman, the original 1943 shooting script
House of Frankenstein, the original 1944 shooting script
The Mummy, the original 1932 shooting script
The Mummy's Curse the original 1944 shooting script (as Editor in Chief)
The Wolfman, the original 1941 shooting script
Dracula, the original 1931 shooting script
House of Dracula, the original 1945 shooting script

CLASSIC COMEDY FILMS
Abbott & Costello Meet Frankenstein, the original 1948 shooting script

CLASSIC SCIENCE FICTION
This Island Earth, the original 1955 shooting script
The Creature from the Black Lagoon, the original 1953 shooting script (editor-in-chief)

THE ACKERMAN ARCHIVES SERIES - LOST FILMS
The Reconstruction of London After Midnight, the original 1927 shooting script
The Reconstruction of A Blind Bargain, the original 1922 shooting script
The Reconstruction of The Hunchback of Notre Dame, the original 1923 shooting script

CLASSIC SILENT FILMS
The Reconstruction of The Phantom of the Opera, the original 1925 shooting script

FILMONSTER SERIES - LOST SCRIPTS
James Whale's Dracula's Daughter, 1934
Cagliostro, The King of the Dead, 1932
Wolfman vs Dracula 1944
Lon Chaney as Dracula/Nosferatu
Robert Florey's Frankenstein 1931

AS EDITOR
Countess Dracula by Carroll Borland
My Hollywood, when both of us were young by Patsy Ruth Miller
Mr. Technicolor - Herbert Kalmus
Famous Monster of Filmland #2 by Forrest J Ackerman

FILM DOCUMENTARIES
A Thousand Faces - as contributor (Photoplay Productions)
Universal Horrors - as contributor (Photoplay Productions)

Mr. Riley has also contributed to 12 film related books by various authors
as well as numerous magazine articles and received the Count Dracula Society Award
and was inducted into Universal's Horror Hall of Fame

Robert Florey's
FRANKENSTEIN
Starring
Bela Lugosi

An Alternate History for Classic Film Monsters

by

Philip J. Riley

Hollywood Publishing Archives

Published by:
BearManor Media
P O Box 71426
Albany, GA 31708
Phone: 760-709-9696
Fax: 814-690-1559
books@benohmart.com

©2010 Philip J Riley
For Copyright purposes
Philip J Riley is the author in the form of this book

Bela Lugosi name and likeness are trademarks of Lugosi Enterprises
Script by Robert Florey and Garret E. Fort, 1931
Cover Art - ©2010 By Philip J Riley - Since none of the scripts in this series were thought to exist and were never produced, we have created mock-up posters in the vintage style of the period.
All photographs are from the Author's collection unless noted
Cover - Jack Pierce's sketch of Lugosi as Frankenstein's monster courtesy Douglas Norwine

The Author would like to thank the following individuals who contributed and helped make this series possible. Carl Laemmle Jr., R.C.Sherriff, Stanley Bergerman, Gloria Holden, Jane Wyatt, Otto Kruger, Marcel Delgado, Robert Florey, Paul Ivano (Cinematographer), Paul Malvern (producer), Elsa Lanchester, Merion C Cooper, Patric Leroux, Bette Davis, Bela G. Lugosi, Sara Karloff, Technicolor Corporation, John Balderston III, Douglas Norwine, Loeb and Loeb Attorneys, David Stanley Horsley, Bernard Schubert, John Teehan, Gregory Wm. Mank, George Turner, Ernest B. Goodman, Universal Legal Department.

Author's Note: I interviewed the producers, directors, stars, cast and crew in the early to late 1970s. They were recalling events that happened 35-45 years previous and sometimes memory fades or events are recalled from their perspective point of view.

First Edition
10 9 8 7 6 5 4 3 2 1

The purpose of this series is the preservation of the art of writing for the screen. Rare books have long been a source of enjoyment and an investment for the serious collector, and even in limited editions there are thousands printed. Scripts, however, numbered only 50 at the most. In the history of American Literature, the screenwriter was being lost in time. It is my hope that my efforts bring about a renewed history and preservation of a great American Literary form, The Screenplay, by preserving them for study by future generations.
For a complete listing of the works of Robert Florey and Garrett Fort see: www.imdb.com

Recommended reading - Robert Florey, The French Expressionist by Brian Taves; Scarecrow Press 1987

This volume is Dedicated to:

Robert Florey

Robert Florey with actress Gail Patrick

And Garrett Fort

Introduction

June 3, 1975

Dear Phil Riley,

    Erroneously, Arthur Lennig wrote in his book " The Count " recently published, that while making the Frankenstein test, in 1931, Bela Lugosi wore a wig with long bushy black hair. This is wrong. Jack Pierce made Lugosi up exactly as he made up Karloff, as the monster, later on. You do not need to visit me with an artist with a picture of Lugosi already sketched - simply look at the Universal film in which Lugosi was the monster, I believe that it was directed by Rowland V. Lee in 1939 and titled " Son of Frankenstein". Karloff was also in it. In the test we made, Bela Lugosi wore exactly the same make up, my only contribution to it being the addition of a couple bolts on both sides of the monster's neck! Some photos of Lugosi as the monster have been published in different books and can be found.

    Arthur Lennig is a professor of film at the State University of New York in Albany. His book is more about Lugosi's films than his life, although Lennig did go to Hungary and dug up quite a bit of information about Lugosi's early days as a leading man on the Budapest stage. But instead of fabricating his story about the Lugosi Frankenstein test and going to Hungary, the author should have come to Los Angeles and had contacted either myself or the man who photographed the test, chief cameraman Paul Ivano who lives at 13.120 Moorpark Sherman Oaks, California. Paul Ivano was the director of photography of several J. von Sternberg productions, he started in the business with Max Linder in 1919 and was the collaborator of such stars as Alla Nazimova and Rudolph Valentino. For many years at the "U" he also photographed some of the Sherlock Holmes others.

    Mae Clarke couldnt hardly remember a thing about the Frankenstein as she was not in it. She was selected by Whale much later.

    Van Sloan played an important part in the test.

    As you say, I am a little tired of hearing about the Frankenstein test It happened forty four years ago - took but two days to make - and I have directed hundreds of cinema features and TV shows since then - I have told and retold all I knew about this test and Paul Ivano gave an interesting interview to a french magazine - a few years ago - regarding the shooting of the test involving a full sequence or about twenty pages of my original screenplay, it was not reproduced over here or at last not given much publicity, perhaps you should see him - in any case he would confirm that Lugosi and Karloff wore an identical make up, created by Jack Pierce, while testing - and later playing - the part of the monster. The Cocoanuts made 47 years ago at the N-Y Astoria studio was a static film - neither the cameras nor the microphones could then move, we were just experimenting.

    Universal - also the other studios - couldnt afford to keep rolls of tests in storage very long - it took too much place - when no longer needed, after a period of a few months they were burned and I suppose that at the time they had no special reason to keep the Lugosi-Frankenstein test, Whale having refused to use Lugosi in the part of the monster.

    Truly Yours,

Robert Florey

A scene from Murders in the Rue Morgue, (1931) directed by Robert Florey and starring Bela Lugosi in place of their original project - Frankenstein

With the success of Dracula, starring Bela Lugosi, Universal Pictures was quick to capitalize on creating a new Lon Chaney in Bela Lugosi. Chaney had been the original choice to portray a duel role as both Dracula and Professor van Helsing, Dracula's adversary. Before production could begin Chaney died suddenly leaving Carl Laemmle Jr. without a star.

Laemmle Jr. had seen Dracula on the stage in New York City, although he could not recall if he had seen Lugosi or Raymond Huntley in the role of Count Dracula. However Lugosi was performing in the touring company which happened to be in Los Angeles at that time. Was he the new Lon Chaney?

Lugosi was not Carl Jr's first choice for the role. However he eventually won the part and now they needed more ideas for him. "Murders in the Rue Morgue", "Cagliostro", "The Invisible Man" and "Frankenstein" were top on the list.

One day in March 1931 Robert Florey, recently returned to Hollywood from Europe, was having lunch at the Musso and Frank Restaurant on Hollywood Boulevard. He was approached by an old acquaintance, Richard Schayer, head of Universal's story department. Schayer told him that his studio was looking for ideas for a new horror film to star Bela Lugosi and he knew Florey was involved with The Théâtre du Grand-Guignol de Paris, (a small theater, in an obscure alley in Paris which specialized in sadistic, shocking, explicit, violent melodramas and became known as the "Theater of Horrors". It opened in 1897 and closed in 1962.)

They both agreed on "Frankenstein" being the best choice. Schayer suggested that Florey would stand a better chance at being asigned writer and director if he were to present the idea to Carl Laemmle Jr.

In his 1948 book "Hollywood d'hier et d'aujourd'hui", Florey described this meeting.

9

"During the course of a singular interview, while Carl Laemmle, Jr. was delivering his fingers to a manicurist, his hair to a hairdresser, his thoughts to his secretaries, and his voice to a dictaphone, I explained to him the general plan of the film. He asked me to quickly type up my story and give it to the head of the scenario department."

Within a month, Florey wrote a five page treatment of the story line. It was approved and Florey was given a contract to write and direct a movie for them.

Even though Dracula's success saved the studio in the midst of the depression Universal still had to close down temporarily, cancelling all productions as well as the studio Exhibitor's newspaper, "The Universal Weekly". Florey continued working on Frankenstein however and when the studio opened about a month later he was teamed up with Dracula's screenwriter Garrett Fort to complete the script.

Garrett Elsden For was born June, 5, 1900 in Jersey City, New Jersey. He began his career as a writer of short stories and playwright.

He made his screenwriting debut with, *One of the Finest* (1917). While working on his silent films he co-wrote the Broadway play "Jarnegan" in 1928.

Fort's first talkie was Rouben Mamoulian's *Applause* in 1929. He is best remembered for his work on the screenplays of *Dracula* and *Frankenstein*.

Deeply troubled throughout his life he sought to find some spiritual fulfillment with the Indian guru Meher Baba and even travelled to India in 1937. But his depression still haunted him and he died of an overdose of sleeping pills in his Beverly Hills apartment on October 26, 1945.

Florey said in 1971, "The only guidelines I had was the Balderston play written in April of 1931 and my own devises. (Balderston had Americanized the British stage production by Peggy Webling.) I wrote the script and (Garrett) Fort would revise my dialogue, at my suggestion. It was written under the impression that Bela Lugosi would portray Henry Frankenstein, but Lugosi was soon assigned the role of the monster."

The first draft script was turned in to the copy department in May of 1931 - with Florey's additions and suggestions added for the next few weeks.

Then another false start occurred. After Laemmle decided that Lugosi should play the Monster, not the Doctor. He asked Florey to direct a "test reel" so that they could make their final decision.

After a day of rehearsals the test was made on stage 12, June 16-17, using the sets from Dracula, at the base of the stairway from its final scenes, Florey made an impromptu laboratory. The first part of the test footage consisted of Victor Moritz's visit to Dr. Waldman and his request for help in getting Henry away from his work. The second reel involved the stealing of the brain by Fritz (Dwight Frye) who comes down the stairs with Dr. Frankenstein holding it in a jar. The creation of the monster with an elixir rather than the full Kenneth Strickfaden electrical devices. Henry Frankenstein and Victor Moritz were played by two unnamed contract players at Universal.

Paul Ivano was chosen as the cinematographer. He had worked for Florey in France on *The Life and Death of 9413, a Hollywood Extra* (1928) (uncredited)

Paul Ivano was born in Nice, France in 1900. He began his career in 1922 as an electrician and camera man for such notables as Eric Von Stroheim, Rudolf Valentino, Nazamova and was first or second cameraman on such films as Greed (1924), and Ben Hur, (1925; 4 Devils, (1928), Queen Kelley, (1929) before being assigned Frankenstein by Florey.

Paul Ivano, cinematographer circa 1930s

Paul Ivano (Cinematographer with Forrest J Ackerman 1974

Ivano recalled that " . . . the test had numerous bizarre angles creating a nightmare atmosphere which was a rather rare thing for that time. Dr. Frankenstein and his assistant descended in the staircase, our mitchell camera had been placed in the center and front of the table where the monster was stretched out lifeless. All of the lighting came from above These trials were so successful, so beautiful, that all the directors of the studio wanted to make the film. Lugosi looked very much like the Karloff makeup that was eventually used in the final film. Lugosi's part in the footage was limited to raising his arm and pulling away the sheet which covered his face and shoulders." (Paul Ivano couldn't remember if he had kept a copy of the test but was sure that he had a few frames stored in his garage in 1972 - but they could not be found)

Lugosi's makeup was designed by Jack Pierce, Universal's chief makeup artist. (as seen in the cover mock-up poster containing Pierce's actual sketch. But as far as the application of the make up Pierce stated that Lugosi rejected it and insisted on applying his own designs; that it was very hairy and tended to melt and run during the walk from the dressing room to the sound stage. (Pierce occupied Bungalow number 5, the former dressing room for the late Lon Chaney)

The novel by Mary Wollstonecraft Shelley give this description of the monster.

"It was a dreary night of November, that I beheld the accomplishment of my toils. . . with an anxiety that almost amounted to agony, I collected the instruments of life around me, that I might infuse a spark of being into the lifeless thing that lay at my feet. It was already one in the morning; the rain pattered dismally against the panes, and my candle was nearly burnt out, when by the glimmer of the half extinguished light, I saw the dull yellow eye of the creature open; it breathed hard and a convulsive motion agitated its limbs.

"How can I describe my emotions at the catastrophe, or how delineate the wretch whom with such infinite pains and care I had endeavoured to form? His limbs were in proportion, and I had selected his features as beautiful. Beautiful! - Great God! His yellow skin scarcely covered the work of muscles and arteries beneath; his hair was of a lustrous black, and flowing, his teeth of a pearly whiteness; but these luxuriances only formed a more horrid contrast with his water eyes, that seemed almost the same colour and the dun white sockets in which they were set, his shrivelled complexion and strait black lips."

The only other references that they had for the monster, at the time, were Edison's *Frankenstein* from 1910, Hamilton Deane in the Peggy Webling play in London and Paul Wegener's, *The Golem*, (1920). All three monsters had long hair. So it would be reasonable to assume that everybody's memories; those directly associated with the 2 test reels, should be combined to make a complete picture.

Ivan Butler rememberd that Deane's stage facial makeup was a light green, with reddish brown distorted lips and a long matted wig.

Edward Van Sloan who acted in the test reels told Forrest J Ackerman that Lugosi looked like something from Babes in Toyland, or like the Golem.

Carl Laemmle Jr. could only recall that he didn't approve of the makeup for the monster, but loved the atmosphere of the test.

The last known picture taken of Edward van Sloan - courtesy - Douglas Norwine

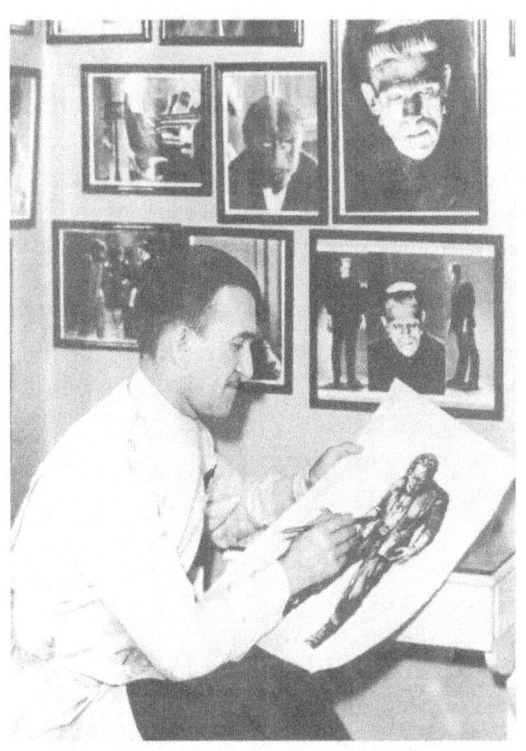

Jack Pierce sketching his version of the monster.

Paul Wegener in The Golem, 1920, one of several possible sources for the test footage makeup.

Mockup Poster *from the 1910 Edison film. This creature and the stage version by Hamilton Deane, Plus The Golem, starring Paul Wegener were the only reference points for the Monster's make up for the test footage.*

The Golem, 1920, a reference point for Frankenstein?

Hamilton Deane as Frankenstein with Dora Mary Patrick from the Little Theatre Production of the play. Naming the classic Universal monster as Frankenstein began in both the London and USA stage.

Hamilton Deane as "Frankenstein."—All photos courtesy of Ivan Butler, who portrayed Victor in this original stage production of 1930

Bela Lugosi, 1931

HOLLYWOOD, CAL. REPORTER
APRIL 29, 1931

Lugosi Signs With "U" On Long-Term Contract

Bela Lugosi has been put under a long-term contract by Universal. He will put on the make-up for Universal's "Frankenstein," after which he will do the leading role in "Murders in the Rue Morgue," adapted from Edgar Allen Poe's short story of the same title.

RECORD APRIL 22, 1931

BELA LUGOSI came back to a surprise after three weeks spent in Honolulu with "The Black Camel" company. His manager signed him on an advantageous long term contract with Universal while he was away. He starts immediately on "Frankenstein," which will be followed by "The Murders in the Rue Morgue." By the time these two are finished the reading department expects to have some more horror tales run down for the man who made "Dracula" a household word.

JUNE 20, 1931

Bela Lugosi begins work soon on "Frankenstein," playing the name role at Universal. He is now studying makeup for the part.

APRIL 25, 1931

... George Melford will direct "Frankenstein"; Bela Lugosi is the star ...

Bela Lugosi Bela Lugosi was next to play "Frankenstein" but he told Carl Laemmle, Jr., that he figured physically he was not strong enough to give the strength and power to the characterization and begged to be given another; this was done, and he was given "Murders in the Rue Morgue" while Boris Karloff played "Frankenstein" and immediately became a star.

L.A. RECORD JUNE 7, 1931

SOMETHING has got to be done for Bela Lugosi. Lugosi has been trying for a week to make a screen test for "Frankenstein." He has to wear a weird makeup, with two or three different colors, stripes, streaks and striations.

But after a few blasts of hot air, the makeup all fuses together, making him a clown instead of a menace.

short picture at a cost of $100 and had all the picture industry interested, is to direct "Frankenstein." This should really belong to Charlie Chaplin, for Bela Lugosi, the star, speaks never a word in the picture.

Actual clippings from Bela Lugosi's personal scrapbook - Courtesy Forrest J Ackerman

                              HENRY

Beast!
     (Hit's him)
Stand quiet. Now speak, slave, speak. Tell this man your
name.
                              MONSTER

     (Sullenly)
Frank-en-stein

                              VICTOR

     (gasps)
Frankenstein!

                              HENRY

Yes, Frankenstein - I made him, I gave him life, he's the
emanation of my brain - - isn't it appropriate that I call him
Frankenstein?

                              FRANKENSTEIN

     (timidly)
Master - made - - ?
        (Unable to express his idea, he thumps
         chest again)
- - made - Franken-stein?

The name "Frankenstein" became attached to the Monster instead of the Doctor as a result of this scene from the play "Frankenstein" by John L Balderston, 1931

As things worked out, Florey didn't get to direct Frankenstein. An English director, James Whale had done so well with Universal's *Waterloo Bridge* that Junior Laemmle felt disposed to offer him any; script he fancied. He chose "Frankenstein".

Upon notification of this change, Florey went back to his contract and saw that he had indeed been hired to write and direct a picture, but there was no specific title mention. There was nothing that he could do but accept a different project, one that he had already begun to outline, *Murders in the Rue Morgue*. Then Bela Lugosi had asked to be let out of the project, stating to Laemmle that he was not physically able to portray the mute Monster. He too was assigned to *Murders in the Rue Morgue*.

Both Robert Florey and James Whale screened *The Cabinet of Dr. Calagari* (1919) and both said they wanted Frankenstein's staging to have a similar look.

The most pronounced ideas that survived to the final shooting script are; First, that Frankenstein accidentally places the brain of a murderer in the Monster's skull. The Second is the windmill in which the Monster perishes in a fire at the end. Florey said that the idea came to him because his Hollywood apartment on Ivar Street overlooked one of the Van de Kamp bakeries, which had a large windmill with wings that turned by mechanical power. Frankenstein's laboratory was situated in the windmill. In the final film the laboratory is located in a ancient tower, much like the laboratory in *The Magician* (MGM 1926) And a line of dialog in reference to the "laboratory" was missed by everyone in the Whale version; where at one point the Baron says: "Why does he go messing around in an old ruined **windmill** when he has a decent house, a bath, good food and drink, and a darned pretty girl to come back to - huh?

The script that you are about to read will show the major contributions of Florey to the project and I recommend viewing the 75th Anniversary DVD release available on Universal Home Video, which is missing only a few minutes of footage, from the graveyard sequence in the opening and several closeups of Fritz as he tortures the monster.

Too late for the American release, Universal finally acknowledged Florey's contribution to the script and he was given writer's credit on the foreign release posters.

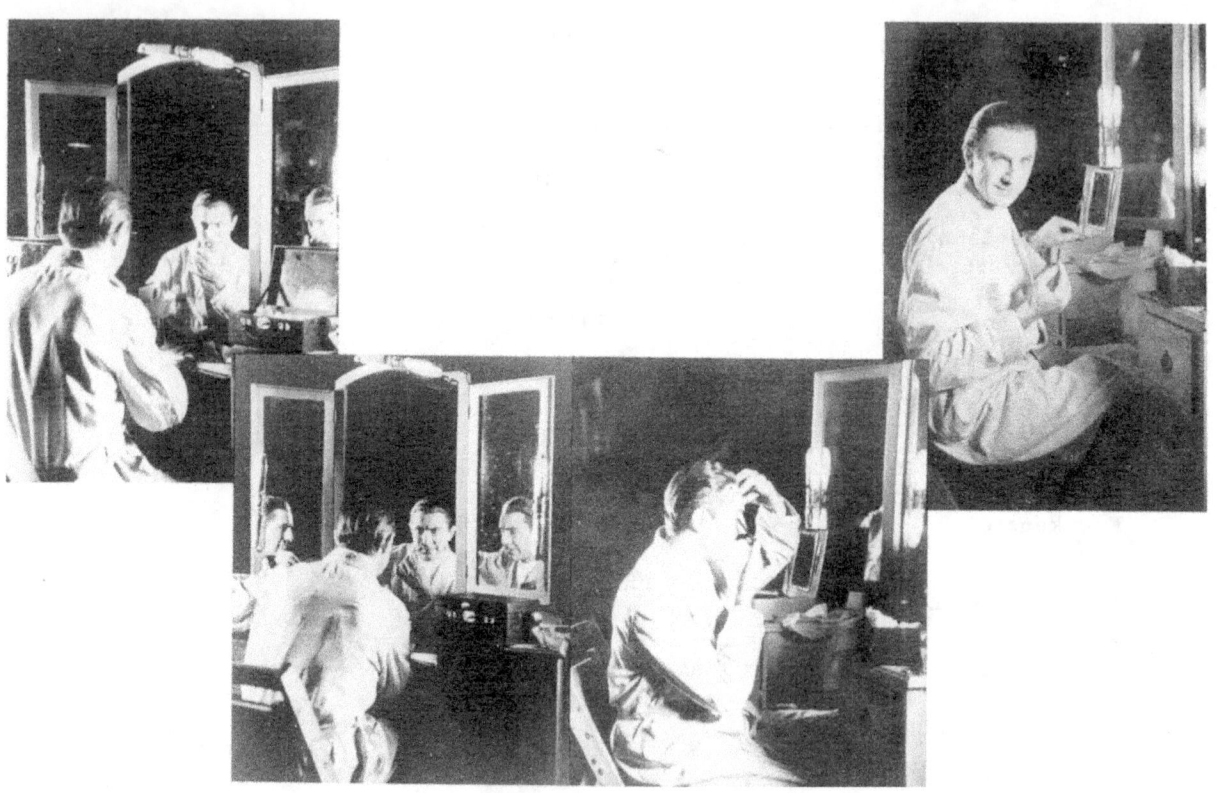

Four publicity shots of Bela Lugosi applying makeup for Dracula - as he was being groomed to be the next Lon Chaney - according to Jack Pierce Lugosi did his own makeup for the test footage for Frankenstein

An original lobby card from the Whale/Karloff version shows that Pierce's makeup even went through changes - Note the clamps holding the monster's flat head to the rest of it's skull

Two French posters, (above and opposite page) of the period that give Robert Florey Screenwriter's credit for Frankenstein

Nurses will be in attendance if you should need their help during the reading of this script!

FRANKENSTEIN

By

Robert Florey
&
Garrett Fort

(May 23, 1931)

Charles D. Hall's original set design of the opening funeral scene (above)
(Below) Hall's design for the ending where Frankenstein dies in the old Mill with his Monster

SEQUENCE " A "

MH

FADE IN: (SOUND: DEEP BELL, SOLEMNLY TOLLING)

A-1   EXT. EXTREME LONG SHOT - HILLSIDE - DUSK

The sun has just set behind a line of poplars which stand sentinel-like, in silhoutte against a cloud-streaked sky.

At the summit of the hill are four rude crosses, tilted at crazy angles, giving the suggestion of a small and ancient cemetery)   (TOLLING OF THE BELL CONTINUES)

Toward these crosses slowly toils a little band of peasants, about eight in all, four of which bear a coffin upon their shoulders.

DISSOLVE THROUGH TO:

A-2   EXT. HILLSIDE - CLOSER SHOT

as peasants pass laboriously up the hill. The pall-bearers are stalwart peasant types, in Central European garb: the others are bent with age, their sharp, hawk faces seamed and lined like withered apples.

An old crone leads a sober-eyed wondering child by the hand.   (TOLLING OF BELLS CONTINUES)

CAMERA PANS SLOWLY WITH THEM, as they move on past the trees, the late sun casting their moving shadows upon the hillside.

DISSOLVE THROUGH TO:

A-3   EXT. TOP OF HILL
In immediate fore., Bulking large against the camera stands the grim silent figure of the gravedigger, leaning upon his shovel, BACK TO CAMERA   (TOLLING OF BELL CONTINUES, SLIGHTLY DIMINISHED)

(CONTINUED)

A-3 (CONTINUED)

    Beyond him, shooting down the hill, the bent figures of the peasants are seen approaching.

A-4   EXT. CEMETERY - MED. SHOT
NEAR WALL

    The wall is quite low, of crumbling stone. One or two forgotten graves with weather-beaten headstones lie in the tall grass just within the wall, swept by the faintly-stirring branches of a willow-tree. To the right of these graves in a break in the wall where a couple of the old stones have fallen in, and through this break, we catch a fleeting glimpse of a man, watching with a furtive air.   (TOLLING OF BELL

    CAMERA MOVES SWIFTLY FORWARD TO CLOSE SHOT OF HENRY FRANKENSTEIN, crouching on the other side of the wall, only his head and shoulders visible.   CONTINUES THROUGHOUT

    He is about thirty, and evidently of a high type of intelligence, but with the glittering eye of a fanatic.   THESE SHOTS;

    As CAMERA PAUSES, the pinched face of a dwarf appears below his shoulder level, also watching.   GRADUALLY DIMINISHING

    AS

A-3   EXT. CEMETERY - MED. SHOT   - INDICATED).

    as the four pall-bearers lower the coffin into the grave. The others stand around in somber silence.

A-6   EXT. FLASH CLOSE SHOT - OLD CRONE AND CHILD

    The old crone, bent almost double with age and infirmity, stands watching the ceremony with an expressionless face, as she fumbles with a rosary suspended around her wrinkled neck.   (CONTINUED)

A - 6   (CONTINUED)

    Beside her, clinging
    to her tattered skirt
    the child glances around
    at her elders with bright
    inquiring, uncomprehending
    eyes.

A-7   EXT. FLASH CLOSE UP -
       OLD MAN

    A fine type of patriarch,
    bowed under the weight of
    the years, wrinkled and
    [toothless, his filmy eyes
    vague as he stands erect,
    his gaze moving slowly from
    the open grave at his feet
    to the sky above.

A-8   EXT. FLASH - SUNSET SKY

    A single star burns brightly
    against the crowing dark.
    Across the sky darts a flock
    of swallows, wheeling into
    the sunset.

A-9   EXT. FLASH CLOSE UP-
       OPEN GRAVE

    as the grave-digger's shovel   (TOLLING
    starts piling earth into
    the hole.   OF

    DISSOLVE THROUGH TO: BELL

        CONTINUES
A-10   EXT. FLASH LARGE CLOSE UP -   TO
       OPEN GRAVE

        DIE
    new filled. The back of the
    shovel is patting the loose   SOFTLY
    earth into a little mound.

        AWAY).

A-11   EXT CEMETERY - FLASH CLOSE
       SHOT AT WALL

    Frankenstein and dwarf watching.
    Lights dim slowly down for sug-
    gestion of coming night

A-12   EXT. CEMETERY - FAIRLY
            WIDE ANGLE - REVERSE SHOT

            with grave in fore., as
            peasants file slowly off
            down the hill in the thicken-
            ing dusk. Lights continue
            to dim.

A-13   EXT. MED. CLOSE SHOT AT WALL

            Frankenstein, following the
            progress of the peasants'
            departure, now raises himself
            slowly to his feet, and stands
            for a moment staring after the
            departing mourners. Then he
            turns to the dwarf, who has
            also risen to a standing pos-
            ition and says sharply:

                                FRANKENSTEIN
                            All right - come along!

            He vaults nimbly over the
            wall, and with a quick back-
            ward glance at the dwarf,
            strides off towards the grave.

            The dwarf brings a pick and
            shovel into sight and, climb-
            ing laboriously over the wall,
            follows him.

A-14   EXT. CEMETERY-MED. SHOT -
            REVERSE ANGLE

            Grave in fore., as Frankenstein
            and the dwarf emerge with swift
            stealth from the shadow of the
            willow-tree and advance to the
            grave.

            Arriving in fore., Frankenstein
            glances about nervously - dwarf
            a little behind him, clumsily
            lugging the pick and shovel.
            Frankenstein snaps:

                                FRANKENSTEIN

                                quick - quick!

(CONTINUED)

A-14 (CONTINUED)
As he says this, he snatches the pick from the dwarf, and kicks it into the newly-covered grave. The dwarf starts to dig with the shovel. As he does so, CAMERA PANS SWIFTLY TO CLOSE SHOT OF ADJOINING GRAVE, a few feet away.

(SOUND OF PICK AND SHOVEL OVER THE SCENE)

This grave is quite modern in appearance and considerably more prestentious than the others, evidently the last resting-place of some important figure in the town.

At the head of the grave is a carved image of Death, shrouded in a robe with a deep cowl - the face invisible, the arms crossed. At first the outlines are dim and vague - then a faint ray of light commences to steal over it, brightening, widening, and we hear Frankenstein say:

> FRANKENSTEIN
> Moonrise - not a moment to lose -

As he speaks, the moonlight steals slowly over the figure, revealing it fully - an impressive, somber witness to the discretion in progress nearby. There is an unspoken menace in its sinister immobility, in the dark shadows which hide the cowled face.

A shovelful of loose earth is hurled into scene - we hear the sound of labored breathing as Frankenstein and the dwarf redouble their hurried efforts.

(SOUND OF PICK AND SHOVEL THUD OF EARTH, LABORED BREATHING)

DISSOLVE THROUGH TO:

A-15 EXT. CROSSROADS - MOONLIGHT-CLOSE SHOT

on the white surface of the road, the figure of a hanged man, swinging slightly from the gibbet, is seen in the shadow.

(CONTINUED)

A-15 (CONTINUED)
CAMERA MOVES SWIFTLY
BACK TO LONG SHOT.
revealing the set-up.

Two white roads are divided
by a strip of rocky land
upon which a crude gibbet
has been erected, and from
the gibbet dangles the limp
form of a man, stark against
the sky. The roads are desolate and deserted - a wild
part of the mountains.

From immediate fore., BACKS
TO CAMERA, the dark figures
of Frankenstein and the dwarf
appear and advance towards
gibbet in background.

Dwarf slinks along at his
master's heels, hesitating
at the sight of the gibbet, but
Frankenstein shoves im on
ahead.

CAMERA FOLLOWS, as they
approach the crossroads.
Directly before the gibbet,
Frankenstein thrusts a glittering knife into the dwarf's unwilling hand and indicating
the gibbet, says curtly:

>   FRANKENSTEIN
>
>   Up! Cut the rope!

The dwarf hesitates again,
with an appealing glance at
Frankenstein - then, as he
sees the look of inexorable
command in Frankenstein's
eyes, he takes the knife and
goes reluctantly forward.

CAMERA FOLLOWS - dwarf starts
to shinny up the gibbet, the
knife between his teeth,
CAMERA PANNING UP as he climbs.

When he reaches the top, he
braces himself with his legs
entwined about the gibbet,
and reaches out towards the
cross-piece to cut the rope.
Only the top part of the rope
is seen, the body itself hanging out of sight. Just as the
dwarf is about to cut the rope,
he pauses, and looks down at
Frankenstein

A-16   EXT. CLOSE UP -
        FRANKENSTEIN

   shot from above, his
   face scowling up into
   camera.

                        FRANKENSTEIN

                   Well, fool! Are you afraid?

A-17   EXT. CLOSE SHOT -
        DWARF

   cowed by his master's
   tone. He reaches forward
   and severs the rope with
   the blade. There is a thud
   as the body strikes the
   ground.   (SOUND: THUD OF FALLING BODY)

   The dwarf gazes down,
   wide-eyed with terror.

A-18   EXT. FLASH CLOSE UP -
        FRANKENSTEIN

   as he bends down to
   examine the body (out
   of scene).

A-19   EXT. FLASH CLOSEUP -
        DWARF

   watching

A-20   EXT. LARGE CLOSE UP -
        FRANKENSTEIN

   looking up at the dwarf
   with an expression of
   disappointment and annoyance.

                        FRANKENSTEIN

                   No use - the neck's broken.

   He lowers his eyes
   towards the body on
   the ground, as we

                   DISSOLVE THROUGH TO:

SEQUENCE "B"

B-1   INTERIOR LIVING ROOM CHALET
        NIGHT .. LARGE CU PHOTOGRAPH
        OF FRANKENSTEIN

   resting in an ornate frame on
   a polished table, the flicker
   of firelight across its face.
   The tilt of the head and general
   expression should coincide as ex-
   actly as possible with the
   preceeding CU.

   CAMERA MOVES BACK SLOWLY to
   include ELIZABETH, Frankenstein's
   fiancee, a charming girl of
   twenty wearing a simple dinner
   frock. She is seated before the
   fire on a low divan adjoining
   the table upon which the
   photograph rests. In her hand
   is a letter which she is turning
   over and over in an absent way.
   It is evident that she is under
   a considerable tension. The
   silver chime of a small Swiss   (MANTEL CLOCK CHIMES
   clock on the mantel rouses her   EIGHT)
   and she rises, tossing the letter
   momentarily aside and taking a
   cigarette from a box on the
   table, lights it and stands
   staring thoughtfully down at the
   photograph, puffing nervously.

   CAMERA CONTINUES MOVING BACK
   ACROSS ROOM, revealing it in its
   entirety. It is the living room
   in a large country house of the
   Swiss chalet type, and while the
   atmosphere of the place is one
   of mellowed age, a definite note
   of modernity is struck by the
   smart appointments. At one side
   is a large window, in a
   curtained alcove, leading to a
   balcony which overlooks the
   village street. At the moment
   the curtains are drawn, through
   low windows on the opposite side
   of the room we glimpse a rustic
   terrace with broad stone flagging
   and the suggestion of the moonlit
   waters of a lake beyond.

   As CAMERA MOVES BACK TO INCLUDE
   DOOR IN IMMEDIATE FOREGROUND, a
   maid-servant in near peasant
   attire enters to announce:

                                                   CONTINUED

B-1   (CONTINUED)

                    MAID SERVANT

                        Herr Victor Moritz

VICTOR MORITZ enters briskly. He is a fine-looking youth in his late twenties. From the far end of the room Elizabeth turns to greet him with a smile in which welcome and relief are mingled.

                    ELIZABETH
                      Victor!

                  VICTOR   (ADVANCING TOWARD HER)

                      Elizabeth - -

Maid servant withdraws, closing door. CAMERA FOLLOWS VICTOR as Xes to Elizabeth. She holds out her hands to him.

                  ELIZABETH

                      It's good of you to come

                  VICTOR (taking hands and kiss-
                         ing them lightly)

                      Nonsense - - I've been as anxious about Henry as you have - - and when I got your message it meant only one thing - - news - -

                  ELIZABETH
                      Yes, a letter. In the late Post.
                         (Xes to divan)

                      I have it here.

                  VICTOR (eagerly)
                      From Henry? at last?

Xes to her, CAMERA FOLLOWING. Elizabeth picks up the letter.

                  ELIZABETH

                      No - -

VICTOR looks disappointed

                    - -it's from Doctor Waldman at the University of Goldstadt

(CONTINUED)

B-1   (CONTINUED 2)

        VICTOR (vaguely)

       Doctor Waldman?

        ELIZABETH
       Oh, surely you remember! He's
       quite renowned. Henry
       received his medical degree
       under him - -they've been very
       great friends - -

VICTOR nods, anxious for   (she pauses)
her to get on.

       - - Until - - well - -something's
       happened. I - - this letter

Sinks down upon the divan
with a troubled air.

       - -It's all here - - I wanted to
       ask your advice before showing
       it to Henry's father.

She unfolds the letter
and studies it for a
 moment with an air of
deep perplexity - -Victor
waiting with ill-
restrained impatience

        VICTOR

       But what - -

        ELIZABETH (referring to letter)

       Doctor Waldman says that
       Henry left the University
       about two months ago - -

        (glancing up at VICTOR)

       That was just after our
       engagement was announced - -

        VICTOR (hurriedly, as if the
           subject is distasteful
           to him)

       Yes, I - - remember - -

        (grimly)

       And you've had no word from
       him since!

        ELIZABETH (with a rueful smile)

       Not a message - - not a letter - -
       nothing

B-1   (CONTINUED 3)

> Victor's eyes are fiercely compassionate. It is obvious that he is hopelessly in love with her. Indicating the letter in her hand, he says rather brusquely:

VICTOR

May I see that?

> She hands it to him. He reads it slowly puzzling over it.

"... one of the most desolate parts of the mountains ... abandoned old mill which he has converted into a research laboratory ...secret experiments..."

(looking up, surprised)

Secret experiments?

ELIZABETH

That's what -- frightens me.

VICTOR

Why?

> She does not reply at first, but sits staring into the fire as if hardly daring to give utterance to her fears. Then she says in a low voice, her face still averted

ELIZABETH

The last time we were together he told me that he was on the verge of a discovery that -- that would --

(pauses)

VICTOR

That would what?

B-2   INTERIOR CLOSE SHOT ELIZABETH

as she turns her head slowly
and looks at him full in the
face, her voice hushed with
awe.

                    ELIZABETH

                        --that would make him as
                        great as God.

B-3   INTERIOR FLASH CU VICTOR

reacting to this in
amusement.

                    VICTOR

                        But that's blasphemy! Henry
                        couldn't have meant it!

B-4   INTERIOR MEDIUM SHOT
        Victor stares at Elizabeth
        who rises and starts to
        pace about, deeply troubled.

                    ELIZABETH

                        I don't know what he meant.
                        He wouldn't say any more.
                        He seemed to regret having
                        said that much.

                    VICTOR

                        I can well imagine--!

                            (refers to letter again)

                        "When I encountered him one
                        day in the village and asked
                        if I might visit his laboratory,
                        he glared at me, said he would
                        permit no one to enter there,
                        that I would be extremely
                        unwelcome. His manner was
                        strange--"

                            (breaking off with a frown)

                        I don't like the sound of
                        this.

                    ELIZABETH (miserably)

                        I don't know what to do--or
                        think--the uncertainty--he'd
                        surely have written unless
                        he's ill--or in trouble--

(CONTINUED)

B-4 (CONTINUED)
She drops disconsolately into a chair. Victor makes an involuntary gesture, as if he longed to take her in his arms and comfort her, but restrains himself, returning rather doggedly to his perusal of the letter. There is a momentary silence as he runs his eyes over the handwritten page; then he says determinedly:

     VICTOR

      I'm going to Goldstadt and find out about all this!

Elizabeth glances up with quick eagerness.

     ELIZABETH

      Oh, why can't we all go?--you and I and Henry's father

     VICTOR (cautiously)

      No--it might be better for me to go alone this time--in case of--

       (pauses, allowing the dark implication to die--taps letter significantly)

      Meanwhile, we'll say nothing about this to anyone. In fact--

       (slipping it into his pocket)

      --I'll take it with me, as an introduction to Doctor Waldman. He'll put me in touch with Henry.

     ELIZABETH

      Do you think Henry will see you?

     VICTOR (with a short laugh)

      His oldest friend?

Xes to window overlooking terrace and stands gazing out over the starlit lake.

(CONTINUED)

      It's only a day's journey--I can leave in the morning.

B-4 (CONTINUED 2)

                    ELIZABETH (rising)

                    Oh, I'll be so relieved.
                    So grateful!

She Xes to him, CAMERA FOLLOWING INTO MEDIUM CLOSE SHOT AT WINDOW Victor turns to her with a smile at once gallant and gay.

                    VICTOR

                    That's enough, then, to send
                    me to the ends of the earth
                    for you!

She smiles affectionately at his pleasantry and allows her hand to rest lightly for a moment on his arm. At this casual contact he stiffens, his face suddenly grim - - the smile still on his lips but gone from his eyes. His voice is low, but still good-natured as he says thoughtfully:

                    VICTOR

                    That's where I should go,
                    really - - to the ends of the
                    earth - - and stay there - -

                    ELIZABETH

                    I'm sure I shouldn't like
                    that.

                    VICTOR (still smiling)

                    As if you'd really care!

                    ELIZABETH

                    Of course I'd care! I'm
                    terribly fond of you.

                    VICTOR (whimsically)

                    Fond of me- -good old Victor,
                    good old boy! Throw him a
                    bone - - pat him on the head- -

Detecting a growing undercurrent of bitterness beneath his banter, Elizabeth shakes her head slowly, in quiet reproach.

                    (CONTINUED)

B-4   (CONTINUED 3)

                    ELIZABETH

            Victor, Victor, my heart - - we weren't ever going to talk this way again - -

Their eyes meet briefly - - hers, soft with understanding and pity - - his suddenly old and tired and hopeless. Then he says, very humbly:

                    VICTOR

            I know. I'm sorry, Elizabeth.

                (raising her hand to his lips)

            Good-night - -

                    ELIZABETH

            Good-night

He smiles and exits abruptly from scene. She stands looking after him in sympathetic silence until the door closes, off-scene, and she is alone - - then she turns and stares out across the moonlit lake with grave, thoughtful eyes.

            (SOUND OF DOOR CLOSING)

                    FADE OUT

SEQUENCE "C"

FADE IN TO

C-1 INT. LECTURE AMPHITHEATER UNIVERSITY
MOVING CRANE SHOT

In immediate fore. are breakaway shelves upon which are various scientific instruments - racks of test-tubes, retorts, glass receptacles, etc. - CAMERA is shooting through shelves to amphitheater proper. The room itself is a combination of lecture hall and laboratory, very modern and up-to-date in construction and appointments. On opposite side from shelves a row of tiers recede upward to the wall and almost to the ceiling. The room is in shadow except for a large and powerful drop-light overhanging a dissecting table upon which lies a body. As scene FADES IN two attenddants are in the act of drawing a rubber sheet over the body. A number of students of various types and ages are lounging about, listening to the conclusion of a lecture by DOCTOR WALDMAN, who officiates at the dissecting table and whose voice carries over entire scene. The room is hazy with tobacco smoke, which drifts about the light in languid whorls.

CAMERA MOVES FORWARD, right through the shelves, which part to admit its progress, and throughout ensuing action keeps moving slowly, never pausing until climax of scene is reached.	WALDMAN - - and in conclusion of this lecture, gentlemen, I wish again to emphasize the importance of this brain specimen - one of
CAMERA MOVES FOREWARD, bringing Waldman into close view. He is holding up a large glass jar containing a human brain - CAMERA definitely establishes this jar and its contents as it continues on past and to the lower row of students.	the most unusual examples of the criminally moronic organ which has ever to my attention come here at the university. I am preserving it in the usual manner and recommend a further inspection at your leisure. To recapitulate
CAMERA MOVES ALONG row of students, quietly picking up several diverse types, all in attitudes of close attention - then continues on up tiers, showing a more scattered grouping (most of the students are congregated in the first three rows) - finally swings abruptly to a small window at the back of the row of tiers, set high in the wall, where we see the face of the dwarf peering thru the glass from outside	an optic thalamus which is only one third the normal size - the almost completely undeveloped frontal lobe, the organ of rationalization, showing that the subject completely lacked the power of reasoning. These salient features which check exactly with the case history of the dead man here, record a life of brutality - of violence and murder!

(CONTINUED)

C-1   (CONTINUED)
      As Waldman brings his   WALDMAN (cont.)
      speeches to this emphatic
      close, CAMERA MOVES   (brief pause, then Waldman
      FOREWARD INTO LARGE CU DWARF,
      his nose flattened out
      against the window pane.   And now, gentlemen, the
                                               class is dismissed.
      At the, CAMERA MOVES BACK
      to show shadows of students
      on the rear wall, as they
      rise to their feet and start
      to leave. There is the sound
      of vague movement, shuffling
      of feet, the rising murmur
      of voices.

C-2   INT. ANTEROOM IN UNIVERSITY OFFICE

      A lean, precise-looking secretary
      with thick glasses, is glancing
      over a schedule for the benefit
      of Victor Moritz, who stands be-
      fore him, his hat in his hand, a
      top-coat over his arm.

                                SECRETARY

                                Doctor Waldman's last class
                                for the evening should be
                                over by now - if you'll wait
                                here, I'll go and verify it
                                for you.

      Secretary rises
                                VICTOR

                                Thank you

C-3   INT. HALL OUTSIDE AMPHITHEATER

      Students are filing out, laugh-
      ing and talking as they separate
      and go their individual ways.
      Waldman bringing up the rear
      talking in a low voice to a group
      of three. Beyond, through the
      open double doors, we see the main
      lights have been switched on, and
      the two attendants are cleaning
      up - one is wheeling the dissecting
      table out through door on far side
      of room, etc. Secretary enters
      scene, approaching Waldman, who
      glances up.   (CONTINUED)

C-3 (CONTINUED)

                    SECRETARY

                There is a Herr Victor Moritz
                who wishes to talk to you
                about Henry Frankenstein.

Waldman looks surprised -
hesitates for a moment with
a little frown - then says
slowly.

                    WALDMAN

                Frankenstein .. Show the
                gentleman into my study.

Secretary nods and exits.

C-4 INT. LECTURE AMPHITHEATER
     MED. SHOT

Shelves in immediate fore.
one of the attendants replaces
the jar containing the brain on
a shelf in fore. - then turns and
Xes towards door. As he reaches
the door, on the other side of the
room, he glances around for the
last time, as if to assure himself
that everything is all right, and
then exits, snapping out the lights
from a wall switch. The room is
dim, with only the moonlight streaming obliquely in from the high windows in the opposite wall. By some
lighting device, jar containing the
brain stands out clearly in fore.
Then CAMERA PANS SWIFTLY ACROSS ROOM,
moving up to CLOSE SHOT WINDOW, as
the dwarf, using a small, sharp in-
strument, presumably diamond-tipped,
removes a small section of the window
pane, inserts his hand, loosens the
catch, and pushing the window open,
drops cautiously into the room. As
he starts down the narrow stairs that
divide the semi-circle of the tiers, CAMERA
MOVES SWIFTLY BACK, preceding him a-
cross the room towards the shelves,
pausing with jar in immediate fore.
again, illumined by a pale shaft of
moonlight. Dwarf into scene - reaches
up on his tiptoes and takes down the
jar - then turns and listens with a
stealthy air.

C-5   INT. WALDMAN'S STUDY
      LARGE CU HUMAN SKULL

as it rests on the top of the
desk among a litter of papers
and odds and ends. Waldman's hand
comes into CU, lifts the top of
the skull, which comes off like a
cover, and inserts the bowl of a
well-colored meerschaum pipe.
We see that the skull is used as a
tobacco jar and is half full of
loose tobacco. Victor's voice is
heard as CAMERA MOVES BACK TO MED.
CLOSE SHOT OF WALDMAN and VICTOR,
facing each other across the desk,
Waldman with his back half turned
to camera.

      VICTOR

    - not having heard from him
    for so long, we naturally
    were quite worried - and then,
    when your letter came -

He pauses, looking anxiously
at Waldman, who is absorbed
in the business if tamping down
the tobacco in his pipe. Waldman
nods slowly, in complete sympathy
with Victor's anxiety - then
lights the pipe and says musingly,

      WALDMAN

    A most brilliant young man,
    herr Frankenstein .. yet so
    erratic... Back over his
    career here at the university
    I look with pride - yet for
    his future - I am troubled -

VICTOR (uneasily)

    So I gathered from the tone
    of your letter.

WALDMAN (puffing away at his pipe)

    His researches in the field
    of chemical galvanism - electro-
    biology - were far in advance
    of our theories here at the
    university - in fact, they had
    a stage reached where they
    were becoming - dangerous

      (CONTINUED)

C-5 CONTINUED

      VICTOR

       Dangerous?

      WALDMAN

       It was his ambition to create
       life.

      VICTOR (relaxing a little)

       The ambition of many modern
       scientists, surely -

      WALDMAN (nodding)

       An age-old dream - the ancient
       mystics - medieval alchemists -

      VICTOR (smiling)

       Fantastic, perhaps - but hard-
       ly dangerous.

      WALDMAN (grimly)

       Dangerous as regards our friend
       Frankenstein - to create life
       he wished first to destroy it
       and then recreate - electric-
       ally

      VICTOR

       Well, I'm aware it isn't a
       very popular procedure, but
       after all, in the interests
       of science, what are the lives
       of a few rabbits, a few dogs -?

C-6 INT. LARGE CU WALDMAN

He hesitates for a moment and them, removing the pipe from between his lips, leans slowly forward into the camera, and tapping impressively on the desk with a pudgy forefinger, says,

      WALDMAN

       Frankenstein was only interest-
       ed in human life!

C-7   INT. FLASH LARGE CU VICTOR

reacting to this, a little
blankly.

C-8   INT. STILL LARGER CU WALDMAN
staring fixedly at Victor as
he goes on to explain.

                    WALDMAN

                        The bodies we use in our dis-
                        secting room for lecture pur-
                        poses were not good enough
                        for his experiments - not
                        perfect enough, he said. He
                        wished us to supply him with
                        other bodies in great quanti-
                        ties, so that he could select
                        those parts which suited him
                        best - the heart of one - the
                        brain of another -
                            (pauses-then adds grimly)
                        - the bodies of the newly dead -
                        and we were not to be too par-
                        ticular where - or how - we
                        acquired them!

C-9   INT. MED. SHOT

Waldman with his back to
camera; Victor facing camera,
a look of incredulity in his
eyes.

                    VICTOR

                        But that doesn't sound like
                        Henry!

                    WALDMAN   (simply)

                        You will find him - changed -

Victor sits quite still for
a moment, never once taking
his bewildered eyes from
Waldman's face, apparently
unable to grasp the terrible
significance of what Waldman
has told him. Then, as it suddenly becomes clear, he starts suddenly to his feet, exclaiming:

                        (CONTINUED)

C-9   CONTINUED

> VICTOR
>> Doctor Waldman, I can't believe
>> it! Henry Frankenstein and
>> I were boys together - I -

Breaks off and starts to walk agitatedly back and forth. Waldman watches him quietly, deeply touched by his distress.

> WALDMAN
>> When I convinced him that his
>> demands were beyond reason,
>> he quit the university and de-
>> clared he would a place find
>> where he could work unhampered.

Victor halts in front of the desk, a little desperately.

> VICTOR
>> But doesn't he realize where
>> such extremes might lead him.

> WALDMAN   (shrugging)
>> Without the protection of an
>> authorized medical body -
>> into the hands of the police.

> VICTOR (excitedly)
>> of course! He must be stopped
>> before he's gone too far!

> WALDMAN   (shaking his head)
>> As a friend, I have remonstrated
>> with him by the hour - but to
>> no good -

> VICTOR
>> Where is he now?

> WALDMAN
>> High up on the slopes of the
>> Weissenberg, in an old mill,
>> where he has a laboratory
>> constructed and fitted up
>> himself.

> VICTOR
>> We must go there at once -
>> tonight!   (CONTINUED

C-9   CONTINUED

> WALDMAN   (a little stiffly)
>
>> He has made it offensively clear that no one is welcome - not even his friends.
>
> VICTOR
>
>> I'll make myself welcome, if I have to batter down his door!
>
> WALDMAN   (earnestly)
>
>> You will be doing him a great service if you can from these subjects his mind divert.
>
> VICTOR
>
>> Look here - I may need your support - you'll be doing me a great service if you'll come along -
>
> WALDMAN   (with polite formality)
>
>> I'm sorry.
>
> VICTOR
>
>> His father - his fiancee - myself - we'll all suffer if he comes to grief!
>
> WALDMAN
>
>> As he undoubtedly will.
>
> VICTOR (urgently)
>
>> Will you come? Will you?

Waldman starts to shake his head again, but is moved by compassion as he looks up into Victor's white strained face. Very slowly and deliberately, he knocks out his pipe and then says, with an air of sufferance:

> WALDMAN
>> Very well, I will go with you.

As he rises and Victor grasps his hand gratefully, exclaiming:

> VICTOR
>> Oh, thank you thank you! It means so much to us all -
>
>> FADE OUT

SEQUENCE " D "

FADE IN: (LOW RUMBLE OF DISTANT
THUNDER)

D-1   EXT. VERY LONG SHOT -
        MILL - NIGHT

        The tall structure with
        its great sails, stands
        near the crest of a
        mountain, in a rocky clear-
        ing about a half mile above
        the timber line.

        It presents a gaunt, almost
        spectral appearance, creat-
        ing an effect of desolation
        and abandonment. The sails
        are torn in some places, al-
        though whole enough to pres-
        ent sufficient wind resistance
        to turn them.

        On the sky-line are great
        dark masses of cumulus clouds,
        piling up against the sky.

        A pale flash of distant light-
        ning illumines the cloud form-
        ation for an instant - a storm
        is approaching, but will not
        break for quite a little while.

        DISSOLVE THROUGH TO:

D-2   EXT. MILL - MED. CLOSE SHOT

        shooting on angle from the
        ground to the roof of the
        mill, where a tall aerial
        with antennae has been erected -
        also a series of lightning rods
        of peculiar design. The small,
        dark form of the dwarf is seen
        scuttling about, performing
        some vague business with wires,
        etc.

        DISSOLVE THROUGH TO:

D-3   EXT. ROOF OF MILL - CLOSER
        SHOT OF DWARF
        wires an implements in his
        hands - is busy at work making
        some sort of connection be-
        tween the rods and antennae and
        two main high frequency wires.   (CONTINUED)

D-3 (CONTINUED)
These frequency wires run down into the interior of the mill.

The roof has been reconstructed so that one-half of it slides back, like the rounded dome of an astronomical observatory, and is controlled by a lever inside, which we see later.

The roof is open, and the dwarf is moving about with considerable agility, leaping here and there to ovoid the opening.

The voice of Frankenstein is heard from below, impatiently calling:

                  FRANKENSTEIN

                  Fritz! . . . Fritz!

Dwarf pauses in his operations, and kneeling down at the edge of the opening he looks into the room below.

CAMERA MOVES FORWARD INTO LARGE CLOSE UP, head and shoulders of dwarf in immediate fore., so that, shooting down over his shoulders into the laboratory below, some fifty feet or more, we see Frankenstein looking up, giving directions.

He is wearing a white surgeon's uniform.

                  FRANKENSTEIN

                  Have you finished hooking up those high frequency wires?

Dwarf nods several times making inarticulate sounds that seem to indicate assent.

D-4 INT. LABORATORY - REVERSE SHOT

the head and shoulders of Frankenstein in fore. this time, shooting up to the large opening in the roof to where the dwarf kneels peering down in.

                  (CONTINUED)

D-4 (CONTINUED)
From somewhere beneath the opening, two shining steel rods, placed about four feet apart, rise into the air from a momentarily unseen fixture on floor of laboratory, connecting with the two high frequency wires, that drop down from above.

                      FRANKENSTEIN (sharply)

            All right - come down here, now, and get this ring electrode attached! Hurry - there's no time to be lost!

His manner is peremptory, indicating a high state of nervous tension. The dwarf chatters something unintelligible - then reaches out and, grasping a rope, which trails loosely from the roof, lowers himself with the quick agility of a monkey to the laboratory level.

CAMERA FOLLOWS HIS PROGRESS DOWN, MOVING BACK to assume floor level focus, and we get a general view of the interior of the laboratory.

It is circular in shape, quite large, with no windows. It has two doors, both of solid oak, with great iron bolts - one leading to the main portion of the mill, and the other, somewhat smaller, opening out upon the narrow balcony which encircles the top floor of the mill. Both doors are closed at this time. The lighting is weird and unearthly.

At one side of the room, covering a vast amount of wall-space, is an intricate electrical machine - a glittering, mysterious apparatus with generators, transformers, wave charger, diffusers, a large rotary spark gap, etc. - very impressive looking, as it looms large and forbidding in the gloom of the room.

                            (CONTINUED)

D-4   (CONTINUED - 2)

    In the wall adjoining this machine, are two large levers and a couple of wheels, constituting the apparatus for opening and closing the roof, and for raising and lowering the other principal feature of the room - a long surgical table, built of shining steel, with telescopic legs, which can be manipulated to raise the table to a height of twelve or fifteen feet above the floor level.

    On this table lies a figure covered with a cloth of some shimmering metallic material designed to catch the light.

    It is Frankenstein's creation - the monster of our story - waiting for the mysterious process which will give it life!

    Above the head is a ring electrode with attached insulator, connecting with the high frequency wires; while encircling the body are three or four mercury tubes, one above the other fashioned to follow the general outline of the body.

    At one side is a battered old sofa and a long table, covered with test-tubes and vials - glass graduates - crucicles - a Bunton burner - sheaves of paper filled with notes and minute mathematical calculations.

    The sofa and the table are the only things in the room which look old or out of place - the rest of the room being apparently the vary last work in ultra-modern equipment. In actuality, it is more impressionistic than scientific, and designed to create a feeling of modern scientific "magic" - something suggestive of the laboratory in "Metropolis".

    As the dwarf reaches the floor level, there is a flash of lightning, and a deep roll of thunder, coming nearer.

                                 (CONTINUED)

D-4   (CONTINUED - 3)

    The dwarf drops down at
    Frankenstein's feet and
    crouches there in terror.

    Frankenstein gives him a
    contemptuous prod with
    his foot.

                   FRANKENSTEIN

            Fool! Afraid of the noise!
            It's the spark you should fear -
            the lightning - those millions
            of volts which mean annihilation-

                  (Softly)
            - or, as we shall demonstrate
            tonight - Life!

    He turns abruptly towards
    wheel in wall. CAMERA
    FOLLOWS, leaving dwarf
    behind.

    Frankenstein starts turn-
    ing one of the large wheels.

D-5   INT. LAB - LONG SHOT - ROOF

    shooting up as roof starts to
    close.

D-6   INT. CLOSE SHOT-FRANKENSTEIN

    glancing aloft as he turns the
    wheel. He is disheveled and
    haggard, his surgeon's uniform
    stained with chemicals and look-
    ing as if he hasn't had it off
    for days - his eyes feverish,
    face glistening with sweat.

    As the roof swings back into
    place, he turns from the wheel,
    talking rapidly, in a low voice
    at first, then rising a little
    wildly.

                   FRANKENSTEIN

            And now for it! The great Work-
            ! - the supreme test -

    He crosses towards table,
    CAMERA MOVING BACK TO
    WIDER ANGLE   - madness or genius - men or
                                      masters - yea - gods -

    (CONTINUED)

D-6 (CONTINUED)

　　　CAMERA, MOVING BACK,
　　　picks up table with
　　　body in fore.

　　　Frankenstein stands
　　　staring at it, his
　　　eyes glittering in
　　　fierce concentration.

        FRANKENSTEIN (CONTINUING)
         Son of the elements - born of
         the lighting - fire -

        (SOUND: RUMBLE OF THUNDER)

         Ah, what a magnificent storm
         this is going to be! We haven't
         had one like it for two months!
         And this time we're ready, eh,
         Fritz? - ready -

　　　He pauses and scowls
　　　down at the dwarf, who
　　　is crouched at the end
　　　of the sofa.

         Why aren't you fixing that
         electrode?

　　　Points to ring electrode
　　　above head of table.

D-7 INT. FLASH CLOSE UP-DWARF

　　　chattering fearfully, and
　　　pointing with a skinny
　　　forefinger towards covered
　　　body on table.

D-8 INT. FLASH CLOSE UP -BODY

　　　lying on table, shooting
　　　up, as seen from dwarf's
　　　point of view.

D-9 INT. WIDE ANGLE

　　　Dwarf crouched in shadow by
　　　sofa in fore. - Frankenstein
　　　and table in b.g.

　　　Frankenstein glances from one
　　　to the other, cot comprehend-
　　　ing for a moment.

         (CONTINUED)

D-9   (CONTINUED)

He then steps closer
to the table, laughing
scornfully.

                    FRANKENSTEIN

                         What! Afraid? Of this dead
                         body?

Dwarf nods, chatter-
ing again and crossing
himself.

                         Why, it can't hurt you - it
                         has no life! You yourself
                         helped me assemble it! You
                         worked beside me - cleaned my
                         instruments - drained off the
                         blood as I built it, piece by
                         piece - arms - legs - heart

                              (beckoning)

                         Come! This is no time for
                         squeamishness!

The Dwarf hesitates -
Frankenstein draws himself
up in attitude of stern
command.
                              (sternly)

                         Do you hear?

Dwarf starts to go forward
reluctantly, like a dog
about to be whipped -
CAMERA FOLLOWING HIM INTO
CLOSER SHOT.

Frankenstein lifts a section
of the covering, revealing a
black arm and hand as it
lies stiffly alongside of
body on table - points to it
reassuringly.

                    FRANKENSTEIN

                         See - there's nothing to fear!
                         No blood - no traces of our
                         handiwork, except a few surgical
                         stitches -

CAMERA MOVES FORWARD INTO
CLOSE UP OF FRANKENSTEIN

                              (CONTINUED)

D-9 (CONTINUED - 2)

           FRANKENSTEIN (continuing, as he glances at body)

- Even the final touch - the brain you stole tonight - in its place, all ready to function -

He drops cover with an exultant laugh.

Think of it - think! The brain of a dead man - and now it will live again - in a body I've made with my own hands!

      (Holds up his hands)

My own hands - !

He stares at them musingly for a moment, then wipes them slowly on the front of his uniform, as if unconsciously feeling that they are stained with blood...

The sound of the thunder rouses him to action - he says sharply:

(RUMBLE OF THUNDER)

Quick! Up there and attach that wire! We'll make on last test -

D-10 INT. WIDE ANGLE

matching Frankenstein's last speech, as he turns abruptly from table towards machine in b.g. Dwarf pulls small stool from behind table - clambers up and starts to attach electrode to high frequency wires.

Frankenstein crosses to machine and makes a connection of some sort - from machine comes a faint humming, as of a dynamo, growing louder, little by little - a blue spark shoots across from one part of the machine to another, with a hiss and crackle

(NOISES OF MACHINE HUMMING - CRACKLE OF SPARK)

(CONTINUED)

51

D-10   (CONTINUED)

    Then he moves towards his work table, and takes up a large sheaf of notes.

    Dwarf glances over his shoulder - fussing around with electrode.

    CAMERA MOVES FORWARD TO CLOSER SHOT OF FRANKENSTEIN who is hastily checking up notes, referring to machine and muttering to himself.

                  FRANKENSTEIN   (muttering)

                  Here we are - here we are - Ammeter reading as of yesterday check -
                        (makes hasty notation)

                  -Transformer - increase high frequency voltage - that will do it -

D-11   INT. CLOSE SHOT - DWARF

    as he completes connection of electrode and high frequency wires - gets down from stool and pushes it out of the way - exits from scene towards Frankenstein.

D-12   INT. MED. CLOSE SHOT - NEAR MACHINE

    matching action as dwarf enters scene - plucks at Frankenstein's sleeve, indicating by means of inarticulate sounds and gestures that he has completed his work.

    Frankenstein glances back towards table in center of room.

                    FRANKENSTEIN

                  All ready, eh? Good - fine -

(CONTINUED)

D-12 (CONTINUED)

    He consults the notes again, and then lays them aside - turns to machine.

                FRANKENSTEIN   (Continuing)
                Stand aside - there's a half
                million volts -

Pulls small lever - the room lights blink wildly - hum of the generator sounds more loudly.

Frankenstein starts making connections here and there, pressing buttons, pulling switches, etc. - one by one, the various portions of the machine spring into life.

CAMERA MOVES SWIFTLY FOREWARD TO CLOSE SHOT OF MACHINE

The rotary spark gap goes into action, emitting a snapping, whirling circle of fire - through large plate glass set in center of machine, another wide, blue spark leaps across the gap -

Frankenstein's voice is heard over scene, exclaiming excitedly:

                FRANKENSTEIN
                There it is - there it is -!
                We've got it! Nothing can stop
                us now - !

As he says this, DOUBLE EXPOSE OVER SCENE CLOSE UP OF WALDMAN'S KNUCKLES rapping on outer door below.

                (RAPPING)

Electrical effects halt abruptly as Frankenstein shuts them off - rapping continues, and we hear Frankenstein's voice, in hoarse whisper:

                What's that?

D-13   INT. FLASH CLOSE UP-
        FRANKENSTEIN

        tense, listening

        DOUBLE EXPOSE CLOSE UP
        ON WALDMAN'S HAND AGAIN -   (SOUND: RAPPING LOUDER)
        hold for three or four
        imperative raps, then
        FADE OUT

                        FRANKENSTEIN

                    Someone at the door below!

D-14   INT. FLASH CLOSE UP -
        DWARF
        listening, frightened.

D-15   INT. CLOSE SHOT -
        FRANKENSTEIN AND DWARF

        both listening, Frankenstein
        with his hand on control
        lever.

                        FRANKENSTEIN

                    Who can that be at this time
                    of night?

        DOUBLE EXPOSE CLOSE UP
        OF WALDMAN'S HAND MUCH
        LARGER, as sound of rap-   (SOUND: RAPPING: MUCH LOUDER)
        ping becomes even louder
        and more insistent.

        FADE OUT as Frankenstein
        says:

                        FRANKENSTEIN

                    Sh - h - h - quiet - !
                    They'll go away -

        CAMERA MOVES BACK TO
        WIDER ANGLE, as Franken-
        stein leaves machine and
        crosses softly towards
        door leading to main portion
        of mill - stands with his ear
        to it, listening.

        DOUBLE EXPOSE HUGE CLOSE UP   (SOUND: RAPPING - VERY LOUD)
        OD WALDMAN'S HAND rapping
        with loud determination.

        (CONTINUED)

54

D-15 (CONTINUED)

    FADE OUT as Frankenstein moves irritable away from the door - doesn't know quite what to do.

    Dwarf hasn't budged an inch - stands regarding him with a panic-stricken air. Frankenstein beckons to him - he crosses quickly to door, CAMERA PANNING TO FOLLOW

                      FRANKENSTEIN (rapidly)

                              Tale a lantern - see who it is and tell them to go away - tell them I'm not here - anything. We mustn't be interrupted now -

    Opens the door and pushes the dwarf through it - then partially closes it and stands listening again.

    A flash of lightning and heavy roll of thunder cause him to glance aloft nervously cursing the delay under his breath.
                                          (SOUND - THUNDER)

D-16 INT. MAIN PORTION OF MILL - CLOSE SHOT - TOP OF STAIRS

    These stairs are of worn stone, and curve down around inside of mill, flush with the wall.

    Dwarf picks up lantern standing just outside of door, and starts cautiously down the stairs - CAMERA FOLLOWS HIS PROGRESS, revolving with angle of the stairs - shadow effect on wall as dwarf continues on down with lantern.

D-17 INT. LABORATORY

    Frankenstein listening at door - glances thoughtfully over his shoulder - then closes door and crosses hurriedly to door leading out upon balcony - opens it and steps out - through open door we catch glimpse of ricketty balcony rail - rain and storm with intermittent flashes of lightning across the night sky.

D-18 INT. LOWER FLOOR
OF MILL - TRAVEL SHOT -

picking up dwarf as he
comes down the stairs
and crosses to door,
CAMERA PANNING TO FOLLOW

There is a small wicket in
door - dwarf stands up on
tip-toe, holding lantern
high, and opens the wicket.

CAMERA MOVES PAST HIM TO
CLOSE SHOT THROUGH WICKET,
revealing the faces of
Waldman and Victor, illumined
by the lantern's flickering
rays.

      WALDMAN (in kindly tones)

       It's Doctor Waldman, Fritz -
       with a friend. Let us in.

D-19 EXT. MILL - RAIN -
CLOSE SHOT THROUGH WICKET

Waldman and Victor in large
silhouette, backs to camera.

Dwarf shakes his head emphatically, and makes guttural
sounds of refusal.

      VICTOR (impatiently)

       Come, come! Don't keep us
       standing out here in the
       storm!

Frit's only reply is to
slam the wicket in their
faces.

      VICTOR (incensed)

       Well!

He starts to batter
angrily upon the
door.

D-20 EXT. BALCONY - RAIN

   Frankenstein is lean-
   ing slightly forward
   over the rail, peering
   down through the darkness
   and rain to see who is
   standing below.

D-21 EXT. MILL - LONG SHOT
      DOWN SIDE FROM ABOVE

   Waldman and Victor standing outside in the storm -
   Victor pounding angrily
   on the door and calling
   out:

                    VICTOR

                       Tell him it's Victor Moritz,
                       do you hear?

D-22 EXT. BALCONY RAIL

   Frankenstein straightens
   up at the sound of Victor's
   voice - very surprised,
   troubled - He hesitates
   for a moment as if trying
   to decide upon a course of
   action - then smiles grimly and
   reenters laboratory, crossing
   towards the other door.

D-23 INT. LOWER FLOOR OF MILL -
      CLOSE SHOT - DWARF AT DOOR

   shrinking a little under the
   angry assaults from without -
   doesn't know what to do.

   The voice of Frankenstein
   sounds from above:

                    FRANKENSTEIN

                       Fritz!

   Dwarf turns quickly,
   looking up

D-24   INT. CLOSE SHOT
           TOP OF STAIRS

Frankenstein in immediate fore,- shooting down over his shoulder, far below, we see dwarf with lantern upraised, looking up

                        FRANKENSTEIN
                          (calling)

                    Let them in!

Dwarf turns to obey, Frankenstein still watching.

D-25   INT. LOWER FLOOR OF
           MILL. MED. SHOT

    as dwarf draws the bolts and swings open the door. Waldman and Victor enter, followed by a gust of wind and rain. Victor favors the dwarf with a sour look - dwarf pays no attention to him, but, hastily closes the door, bolting it again. Victor observes this action suspiciously. Waldman, however, remains unperturbed - shakes the rain off his hat, saying to Fritz in gentle reproof:

                        WALDMAN:

                    Keeping us out in all that
                    storm, Fritz - !

Frankenstein's voice greets them mockingly from above.

                        FRANKENSTEIN:

                    A bad night for calling
                    my friends!

Waldman and Victor look up - CAMERA SWINGS UP to L.S. of Frankenstein, high above the top of the stairs. Victor's voice is heard over scene.

D-25   CONTINUED

                  VICTOR

            Henry! What is all this
            nonsense of locked doors and -

        FRANKENSTEIN   (cutting in sharply)

            Come up! Come up!

CAMERA SWINGS BACK TO
MED. SHOT - LOWER FLOOR

Waldman and Victor start
up the stairs, the dwarf bringing up the rear with his lan-
ern. As the strange trio climb
the worn stone stairs, CAMERA
SPIRALS UP with them, the
lantern casting huge, fantastic
shadows on the walls.

DISSOLVE THROUGH TO:

     INT.
D-26 TOP OF STAIRS

Waldman and Victor completing
their climb, Waldman a little
out of breath. Frankenstein
is waiting in the doorway.

                FRANKENSTEIN   (smiling a
                                            wan welcome)

            Victor!

Grasps Victor's hand
impulsively.

                  VICTOR
            Henry, what in the name of -

                FRANKENSTEIN

            And Doctor Waldman! I don't
            deserve your forgiveness -

        WALDMAN   (extending his hand)

            But you have it.

                  VICTOR

            You've had us all frantic -
            Elizabeth - your father -

They proceed into the
laboratory, Frankenstein
and the dwarf bringing up
the rear. Dwarf leaves lantern
outside on the landing.   (CONTINUED)

D-26   CONTINUED

                    FRANKENSTEIN

                         If I have, I'm sorry. When
                         I explain -

DISSOLVE THROUGH TO:

d-27   int. laboratory. reverse shot

matching action as Waldman and
Victor precede Frankenstein into
the room. Dwarf slides in past
the three of them and scuttles
off out of camera to other side
of room. Frankenstein pauses at
the door to close and bolt it-
as Waldman and Victor observe
this with an air of mild inquiry,
he says by way of explanation:

                    FRANKENSTEIN

                         I've been forced to take unu-
                         sual precautions -

                    VICTOR

                         Against what?

                    FRANKENSTEIN

                         I've had spy mania - I've been
                         afraid of people prying about
                         trying to find out things -

Comes forward - CAMERA
MOVES BACK TO WIDER ANGLE

                    VICTOR   (bewildered and impatient)

                         I don't understand all this
                         mystery -

                    FRANKENSTEIN

                         Be patient - you will

Waldman is looking around
him with an air of keep profes-
sional interest at the unusual
equipment and general character
of the room.

                    WALDMAN   (half to himself)

                         Amazing - amazing

                                        (CONTINUED)

D-27 CONTINUED

> He moves away from Victor and Frankenstein, completely absorbed in his inspection of the room with its strange instruments - CAMERA SWINGS AROUND TO CLOSE SHOT VICTOR AND FRANKENSTEIN. Victor has been studying Frankenstein carefully, disapprovingly, as if his worst fears were realized.

VICTOR

> Henry, you're not well - look as if you were on the verge of a breakdown! You must come home at once!

FRANKENSTEIN

> Impossible!

VICTOR   (indignantly)

> But haven't you any regard for anyone's feelings? Your father's? Elizabeth's?

FRANKENSTEIN

> Is that what they think?

VICTOR

> They haven't known what to think! No letters -

FRANKENSTEIN   (passing hand
> over eyes

> I know - I know. I've no excuse but work - but they'll overlook everything when they learn what I've been doing -

VICTOR

> That's just it! What are you doing! This fantastic-looking place

FRANKENSTEIN

> The whole world will acclaim me - tomorrow.

> (CONTINUED

61

D-27   CONTINUED

                    VICTOR   (a little bitterly)

                    The world's acclaim means
                    more to you, then, that
                    Elizabeth -

                    FRANKENSTEIN   (earnestly)

                    No, no - - you don't understand,
                    Victor! I'm doing all this
                    for her - to make her proud -
                    proud -

There is a commotion off-
scene - both turn quickly

D-28   INT. CLOSE SHOT AT TABLE

Waldman, pursuing his invest-
igation of the room, has approached
the table upon which the Monster
lies, and has been about to raise
the covering, when the dwarf, with
a snarl, has leaped between him and
the table, barring the way.

D-29   INT. WIDE ANGLE

   matching action as Frankenstein
   springs forward, crying excitedly,

                    FRANKENSTEIN

                    Waldman! Keep away from that
                    table!

and yanks Waldman's arm back
Waldman look surprised -
a little hurt.

                    WALDMAN   (gently shiding)

                    My boy -

Frankenstein releases his
arm, shamefacedly.

                    FRANKENSTEIN

                    I'm sorry - I meant no offense
                    I -

                         (CONTINUED)

D-29   CONTINUED

    Waldman pats his shoulder tolerantly. Frankenstein indicates sofa - says with an obvious effort at self-control

                        FRANKENSTEIN

              Sit down there, Doctor, please- both of you - let me try to explain.

                        VICTOR

              The sooner the better -

    Waldman Xes obediently to the sofa and sits down, watching Frankenstein closely, with an air of professional interest. Victor takes a position behind the sofa - they both wait for Frankenstein to speak. Frankenstein seems unable to get started - he moves about with quick, nervous movements, cocking his head aloft at a sharp flash of lightning and the resultant roll of thunder. Waldman, as if to help him, tries to lead into the explanation by asking, in matter-of-fact tones,

                        WALDMAN

              What have you there on the table that you don't wish me to disturb?

                        FRANKENSTEIN

              A body.

D-30   INT. FLASH CU VICTOR

    showing unpleasant reaction. Waldman's voice comes calmly ⌐over CU.

                        WALDMAN'S VOICE

              Well - and what are you doing with it?

D-31   INT. MED. SHOT. ANOTHER ANGLE

    matching action as Waldman
    finishes question. Frankenstein
    does not reply at once, but
    resumes his nervous pacing.
    Then he stops in front of Waldman and
    says earnestly, almost pleadingly:

                  FRANKENSTEIN

                You must let me tell you
                in my own way -

        WALDMAN   (gently)

                of course.

Frankenstein nods several
times, his eyes harried -
then braces himself as if
for a terrific ordeal, and
speaking very rapidly, in
cisively, says:

                    FRANKENSTEIN

                Doctor Waldman, for the benefit
                of our unscientific friend
                here -
                      (indicates Victor with
                          a jerk of his head)
                -what is the highest color
                in the spectrum - the last
                color we can see.

        VICTOR

                Violet - even I know that.

Frankenstein nods brusquely,
glad there is no necessity
for further explanation along
these lines. Waldman, a stickler
for scientific accuracy, makes
an amendment:

        WALDMAN

                Science had discovered another
                color - another ray - the ultra
                violet

                    (CONTINUED)

D-31   CONTINUED

      FRANKENSTEIN   (nodding)

    Quite right - common knowledge.
      (pauses and takes deep
      breath)
    Well, I've gone beyond that.
    I've found another ray, hotter
    than the ultra-violet - more
    powerful - life-giving -
      (emphatically)
    -life-creating!

      WALDMAN   (all attention now)

    You have discovered some
    new force?

      FRANKENSTEIN

    The greatest! (steps to machine)
    In this machine are all the
    rays of the spectrum - the
    ultra violet beyond that -
    and beyond that, the Great
    Ray which in the beginning
    brought life into the world!

He brings this speech to a triumphant climax, his eyes gleaming with a almost fanatic light. Waldman stares - there is a momentary silence - then Waldman says, with an incredulous smile,

      WALDMAN

    Come - come - that's a pretty
    wild statement - without proof!

D-32   INT. FLASH CU FRANKENSTEIN

as he utters a sharp, unpleasant laugh and snaps -

      FRANKENSTEIN

    You'll have proof - tonight!
      (indicates machine)
    I'm going to turn this ray on
    the body on that table
      (points to table with
       outstretched arm)
    - and bring it to life!

CAMERA SWINGS AROUND TO CLOSE SHOT BODY ON TABLE, and remains there for balance of speech.

D-33   INT. FLASH CU VICTOR

perfectly certain that his friend has gone out of his mind.

                    VICTOR

                You're insane!

D-34   INT. MED. SHOT

Frankenstein in fore. - Waldman continues to stare at him in stunned silence for a moment - then shakes his head with grave misgiving.

                    WALDMAN

                My boy, my boy, your studies have been too much for you -

He starts to rise. Frankenstein advances towards him a step or two, creating the feeling of almost pushing him back by sheer force of his impassioned speech.

                    FRANKENSTEIN

                You're both wrong! I'm quite sane! I know. I've demonstrated it on lesser forms of life! I brought to life a dog killed by lightning! I had a heart - a human heart taken from a dead man, which I resuscitated and kept beating for three weeks!

Pauses, confronting them with a terrible smile of triumph.

                There! What do you think of that?

He stands before them, drawn up to his full height, quivering with suppressed excitement. Waldman stirs uneasily and looks up over his shoulder at Victor, who has not moved since his last outburst - then back at Frankenstein, his eyes narrowing as he finally finds his voice sufficiently to ask:

                    WALDMAN

                You really believe you can - restore the dead - to life?

D-35   INT. FLASH CU FRANKENSTEIN

    his smile more terrible as he
    replies, softly:

>   FRANKENSTEIN
>
>   The body on that table is not
>   dead. It has never lived!

D-36   INT. FLASH CU WALDMAN

    as he gasps:

>   WALDMAN
>
>   What!

D-37   INT. FLASH CU FRANKENSTEIN

    enjoying the sensation he
    has created - his voice raises
    to a climactic pitch:

>   FRANKENSTEIN
>
>   I created it!

D-38   INT. FLASH LARGE CU WALDMAN

    gaping, speechless.

D-39   INT. FLASH CU VICTOR   (TERRIFIC CRASH OF THUNDER AS
                                             STORM BREAKS OVERHEAD IN FULL
    stiffening in horror   FURY)
    with a sibilant intake
    of his breath.

D-40 INT. FAIRLY WIDE ANGLE

shooting towards Frankenstein
Victor and Waldman in silhouette
in fore., backs to camera
Frankenstein draws nearer,
speaking very rapidly:

                FRANKENSTEIN

           Mad with my own hands -
           assembled organ by organ -
                (to Waldman)
           You remember our quarrel, when
           I quit the University?
                (Waldman nods)
           You thought I was mad, then-
           you refused to find bodies for
           me to use - ! Well, I found
           them - I used them!

Waldman rises very slowly,
back still to camera, his
voice ringing out in stern
accusation as the underlying
meaning of Frankenstein's
words become clear.

                WALDMAN

           Where did you find them?

                FRANKENSTEIN   (grimly)

           Where they had been buried.

                WALDMAN

           You mean you desecrated graves?

                FRANKENSTEIN   (ruthlessly)

           Yes - at first. But those
           who died of disease -

D-41 INT. LARGE CU WALDMAN

regarding Frankenstein with
the cold, merciless eyes of
judgement. Frankenstein's
voice continues, unbroken
over CU....

                FRANKENSTEIN

           -whose life-machines had al
           ready run down like worn-out
           clocks defeated me. Corruption
           set in too soon. I had to
           have perfect organs -

D-42   INT. MED. SHOT

matching action as Victor
and Waldman continue to
stare at Frankenstein, whose
voice continues, unbroken,
from preceding shot.

      FRANKENSTEIN

    - I turned to violent death
    for my experiments! Do you
    remember the body of that
    murderer which hung in chains
    on the gibbet above Goldstadt?

      WALDMAN

    It disappeared -

      FRANKENSTEIN

    I stole it!

    VICTOR (aghast)

    In God's name, Henry - !

      FRANKENSTEIN

    -used what portions I found
    necessary -

He halts, breathless,
unable to go on. Waldman
looks at him without speaking for a moment. Then a
look of pity comes over his
face as he appears to realize
that he is dealing with a man
temporarily deranged, who must
be protected against the con-
sequences of his folly - glances
significantly at Victor and then
back at Frankenstein - says,

      WALDMAN

    We will help you bury the
    corpse - we will keep your
    secret -

    FRANKENSTEIN (laughing unnaturally)

    There's nothing left to bury-
    I destroyed the remains with
    acid!

As he says this, he has apparently reached the end of
his strength - turns abruptly
and Xing to work-table where
his notes, instruments, etc.
lie, and picking up a flask,
pours himself a drink - CAMERA
PANNING TO FOLLOW

D-43   INT. MED. SHOT
       VICTOR AND WALDMAN

   Their heads turn, following
   him in blank dismay and stupe-
   faction - then their eyes seek
   each other's. Both appear utterly
   incapable of words. Frankenstein's
   revelation has overwhelmed them.
   Waldman sinks slowly back down
   upon the sofa and covers his eyes
   with his hands. Victor stands like
   a graven image, nothing alive but   (SHARP CRACK OF THUNDER
   his eyes, which are vivid with help-   SOUNDING DIRECTLY
   less horror. There is a brilliant   OVERHEAD)
   flash of lightning - a crack of
   thunder. They are too dazed to pay
   any heed.

D-44   INT. CLOSE SHOT FRANKENSTEIN

   gulping down his drink - pauses
   in the midst of the act as
   another flash of lightning illum-
   ines his face, which is streaming
   with great beads of sweat. The
   sound of thunder seems to
   open new reserves of energy, as
   he springs into action, shouting:

                   FRANKENSTEIN

               Fritz! Fritz!

   Exits from scene

D-45   INT. FLASH OF DWARF

   who has been huddled on a high
   stool in a corner - he slips
   obediently down from the stool.

D-45   INT. WIDE ANGLE

   matching action as Frankenstein
   Xes in great strides towards the
   table upon which the body lies,
   summoning Fritz with an impatient
   snapping of his fingers.

                   FRANKENSTEIN
               Come! We've not a moment
               more to waste! It must be
               now!
                       (CONTINUED)

70

D-46   CONTINUED

As Fritz Xes, reluctantly but having no choice, towards the table where the body lies, CAMERA MOVES FORWARD INTO CLOSER SHOT. Frankenstein moves about with swift precision, making final examination of the electrodes, wires, etc., checking them aloud:

> FRANKENSTEIN
>
> Everything is ready - the electrodes - wires - all right, Fritz, - all right -

D-47   INT. MED. SHOT WALDMAN AND VICTOR

Waldman looks up slowly, watching Frankenstein's shadow, flitting back and forth from table to machine, passes across the faces of Waldman and Victor. Waldman says nothing for a moment, then asks in a strained voice:

> WALDMAN
>
> What are you going to do now, Henry?

D-48   INT. WIDE ANGLE

Waldman on sofa in b.g. - Frankenstein pauses half-way between table and machine - says tensely:

> FRANKENSTEIN
>
> I'm going to prove my sanity - if you care to remain and watch -
> (pauses, half mockingly)
> Or perhaps you would prefer to leave me alone in my madness -

Waldman rises slowly, drawing a deep breath and saying with an air of helpless resignation

> WALDMAN
>
> I will see this horror through

(CONTINUED)

D-48   CONTINUED

                FRANKENSTEIN (with increased
                                    mockery)

            Excellent! There speaks
            the scientist!
                    (to Victor, who has not
                    moved)
            And you, Victor - ?

     VICTOR   (with an effort)
            Of course - I'll stay -

     FRANKENSTEIN   (with mad gaiety)

            Good! Good! The three of us-
            here in the dark and the storm-
            watching the dawn of a new day
            for humanity - !
                (to Fritz)
            Quick - the wheel - when I
            tell you -

Fritz scuttles across the
room and takes his place
beside the wheel which con-
trols the roof. Frankenstein
again addresses Waldman, his
voice this time a little more
under control - brisque,
businesslike:

                FRANKENSTEIN

            And now, Doctor - if you will
            come here - and satisfy you-
            self that this body is quite
            without life -

Waldman hesitates for a moment
then starts to come slowly forward, as if every step were an
effort. Victor comes around
from behind the sofa, his eyes
still fixed wonderingly upon
Frankenstein's excited, gleaming
face. CAMERA SWINGS AROUND so
that table with body is in immediate fore. - Waldman approaches
and stands looking down at the
body, still covered by the shim-
mering cloth. Frankenstein reaches
down and lifts a corner of the cover -
Waldman makes no move as yet, but
stands gazing down at the body with
an expression of repulsion.

                FRANKENSTEIN

            Test it - thoroughly - there
            must be no doubt.

          (CONTINUED)

D-48 CONTINUED-2

Waldman puts his head down to the chest of the corpse to listen for possible heart action or indications of breathing - his action is quite perfunctory, however, there being little doubt in his mind but what Frankenstein has stated the condition correctly. Then he straightens up and lifts one of the arms into the camera - it is black and rigid - drops it quickly, with a shrug, Victor peering over his shoulder with grim, fascinated eyes.

                    WALDMAN

          Of course the thing is
          dead.

                    FRANKENSTEIN   (raising cover a
                                      little more)

          The face - look at the face -

D-49 INT. FLASH CU FACE OF CORPSE

It is chalky white and expressionless - moulded so as to be just a trifle out of proportions, something just this side of human - but that narrow margin is sufficient to make it insidiously horrible. Waldman's voice, coming over CU in shaky tones, describes it perfectly:

                    WALDMAN

          it is like a death-mask of
          a monster -

D-50 INT. WIDE ANGLE

matching action as Frankenstein drops the cover back into place, exclaiming:

                    FRANKENSTEIN

          Not very flattering to my
          prowess as a sculptor, doctor-
                    (to Fritz, in ringing
                     tones)
          All right, Fritz - the wheel -!

They turn quickly, glancing across the room toward Fritz.

73

D-51   INT. FLASH CU FRITZ

        as he starts to turn the wheel controlling the roof.

D-52   INT. FLASH CLOSE SHOT ROOF

        rolling back. The rain beats in - there is another flash of lightning, followed by a crash of thunder.   (CRASH OF THUNDER REVERBERATING)

D-53   INT. FLASH CLOSE SHOT GROUP

        Waldman, Victor, and Frankenstein gazing aloft - Waldman and Victor with expression of amazement, Frankenstein glancing slyly at them, enjoying their reaction.

D-54   INT. FLASH CU DWARF

        shrinking back at the fury of the elements - releases wheel.

D-55   INT. L.S. ROOF

        completely rolled back - as seen from floor of laboratory.

D-56   INT. WIDE ANGLE

        Machine in fore. - Frankenstein Xes from table towards machine and stands for a moment with his hand on the lever controlling movement of table - cries in warning to Waldman and Victor:

                    FRANKENSTEIN

                    Stand back!

        Presses down upon the lever and stands watching table - Waldman and Victor step quickly back, startled - table starts to move towards roof, the steel telescopic legs unfolding slowly, noiselessly.

D-57   INT. CLOSE SHOT TABLE

as it moves slowly up into
the air - CAMERA FOLLOWING
AT TABLE LEVEL - the figures
of Waldman and Victor pass
down out of scene as table
continues upward.

D-58   INT. L.S. FROM ABOVE

shooting down into laboratory
as table rises slowly into
camera - Waldman and Victor below, looking up.

D-59   INT. FLASH CU WALDMAN'S FACE

looking up.

    d-60   int. flash cu victor's face

    looking up.

D-61   INT. FLASH CU FRANKENSTEIN'S FACE

Looking up - grim-lipped - under
terrific strain.

D-62   LABORATORY

matching action as the men look
up at table - shooting on angle to
include table, which has now risen
to a height of fifteen feet or more
and come to a stop.

D-63   INT. L.S. FROM ABOVE

showing the men looking up at table, which rises into fore. at height of fifteen feet or more and comes to a sudden halt.

D-64   INT. LABORATORY
        MED. SHOT FLOOR LEVEL

as the tension relaxes for a brief moment - Waldman and Victor glance across at Frankenstein, who steps quickly away from the lever towards the great machine nearby. He is greatly excited, jabbering an incoherent explanation as he points aloft, dividing his attention between them and machine.

                    FRANKENSTEIN

                        Antenna on roof - connect
                        with high frequency wires -
                        electrodes on table there -
                        then with this machine -

CAMERA MOVES SWIFTLY FORWARD
INTO CLOSE SHOT FRANKENSTEIN
AT MACHINE

He makes the same connection as in previous scene - generator starts to hum - blue sparks crackle across face of machine - the rotary spark gap emits the same whirling, snapping circle of fire - Frankenstein's voice trails away as he concentrates his entire attention upon machine, which now springs into action, full blast - Frankenstein leaps back, crying:

                        (NOISES OF MACHINE)

                    FRANKENSTEIN

                        Take care! Stand back!

D-65   INT FLASH CU MACHINE

       Electrical effects

       DISSOLVE THROUGH TO

D-66   INT. FLASH CU ANOTHER PART
       MACHINE

       Electrical effects. DOUBLE   (NOISES
       EXPOSE CU FRANKENSTEIN - flash
       of his white, strained face -   OF
       HOLD DOUBLE EXPOSE and
       DISSOLVE THROUGH TO: MACHINE

                                                   THROUGHOUT

                                                   THESE

D-67   INT. FLASH LARGER   SHOTS)
       CU MACHINE

       More effects - CU FRANKENSTEIN
       double-exposed faintly

       FADE OUT DOUBLE EXPOSE

D-68   EXT. FLASH NIGHT SKY

A vivid streak of lightning
across the sky, followed al-
most immediately by sound of   (THUNDER - LOUD)
thunder, which carries over
into next shot.

D-69   INT. FLASH LARGE
        CU MACHINE

electrical effects as preceding
lighting flash effects same   (MACHINE NOISES)
visible reaction.

D-70   INT. FLASH CLOSE SHOT TABLE

electrical effects whirling
in circles around table through   (HISSING SOUNDS)
glass tubes.

D-71   EXT. FLASH L.S. MILL

showing fury of storm - trees
bending wildly - lashing rain -
howl of the wind - a jagged
streak of lightning cuts across
the sky behind the mill, throwing
it momentarily into sharp silhouette.

D-72   INT. LABORATORY, FLASH
        CLOSE SHOT OF WALDMAN AND VICTOR

watching, the lightning on their
faces - weird effects   (MACHINE NOISES VERY LOUD)

D-73   INT. LABORATORY, FLASH CU
        FRANKENSTEIN

        standing near the machine - he
        screams against the noise of
        the machine:

                    FRANKENSTEIN
                We haven't gotten a direct
                connection yet!

        Another flash of lightning
        streaks across his face.

D-74   INT. LABORATORY. FLASH CU DWARF

        shrinking back against the wall
        behind the work table in abject
        terror.

D-75   EXT. L.S. NIGHT SKY

        showing mill and trees again -
        a particularly blinding flash of
        lightning, followed instantly by
        an almost deafening crack of
        thunder.

D-76   EXT. FLASH CLOSE SHOT
        TOP OF MILL

        Lightning contacts with antennae -
        the lightning flashes along the
        high frequency wires blindingly.

D-77   INT. LABORATORY
        FLASH CU DWARF

        as this lightning flash flares
        luridly across his contorted face-
        he screams and buries his head
        in his arms.

D-78   INT. LABORATORY. WIDE ANGLE

as high frequency wires contact
electrodes - great electrical
display as glass rings around   (THUNDER)
table crackle with the intense
heat - entire face of machine
seems to suddenly become blotted
out by a blinding flash of fire.

D-79   INT. FLASH CU FRANKENSTEIN

in negative - 12 frames.

D-80   INT. LABORATORY. WIDE ANGLE

As another terrific bolt of
lightning strikes the apparatus,
(12 frames)

       INT.
D-81   FLASH CU WALDMAN AND VICTOR

in negative - 12 frames   (LOUD THUNDER)

D-82   INT. LABORATORY. WIDE ANGLE

A final and terrific flash of
lightning, completely blotting
out the scene - the crash of
thunder - roar of machine -   (THUNDER - MACHINE NOISES
screams of dwarf - then laboratory   CRIES OF DWARF)
is seen again - every light blown
out - just the outlines of the men
and the pale flicker of their faces
as lightning plays across them,
diminished in fury.

D-83   INT. FLASH ENORMOUS CU WALDMAN

    staring up into the storm.

D-84   INT. FLASH ENORMOUS CU VICTOR

    terrified, also looking up

D-85   INT. FLASH ENORMOUS
       CU FRANKENSTEIN

    completely exhausted, in a
    state bordering on complete
    collapse, also looking up.

D-86   INT. LARGE CU TABLE

    as electrical effects around
    it die out. The hand of the Monster
    is seen dangling over the side
    where it was dropped by Waldman
    in his hasty examination. CAMERA
    MOVES TO LARGE CU HAND, which is
    blank, as before. Then slowly
    the tips of the fingers start to
    turn white - the transition from
    black to white starts to creep up
    the hand towards the wrist until
    the entire hand is white and normal-
    looking. We see for the first time
    that the fingers have no finger-
    nails.

D-87   INT. LABORATORY, FLASH LARGE CU
       DWARF

    peering aloft from within the shelter
    of his arms - suddenly his eyes grow
    wide with fear - he screams in terror
    levelling a trembling finger up towards
    the table

D-88   INT.   FLASH CU HAND OF MONSTER

       as one of the fingers starts
       to move, slowly, stiffly

D-89   INT. FLASH CU WALDMAN
       staring aloft incredulously.

D-90   INT FLASH CU HAND

       as another finger repeats the
       movement - then a third.

D-91   INT. FLASH CU VICTOR

       starting back with a muffled
       cry as he observes the movement.

D-92   INT. FLASH OF CU ARM OF MONSTER

       as it stirs beneath the covers -
       starts to move limply, but with
       growing strength, fingers feebly
       clutching at edge of cover.

D-93   INT. FLASH LARGE CU
       FRANKENSTEIN

       watching this - a look of insane
       exultation spreads over his face -
       his eyes light up - he starts to
       tremble violently - then to laugh, in
       low tone at first, but gradually
       louder and louder.

D-94   INT. FLASH CLOSE SHOT TABLE

over the side we see the white
arm continue to move, getting
stronger - then there is a   (FRANKENSTEIN'S
vague movement beneath the   LAUGHTER FAINTLY
cover, as of a whole body stirring   OVER THE SCENE)
weakly, like a man coming out of
an anesthetic. As Frankenstein's
laughter dies away for a moment, we
hear from beneath the cover a faint
sound- a whimper, like that of an
animal in pain.

D-95   INT. LABORATORY. WIDE ANGLE

at floor level as Waldman and
Victor back away from beneath
the table, Waldman collapsing
upon the sofa. For the first
time they find themselves able   (FRANKENSTEIN'S LAUGHTER)
to speak, Frankenstein is laughing -
louder - louder

                    WALDMAN

                Lights! Lights!

                    VICTOR
                There are no lights!

                    FRANKENSTEIN   (laughing crazily
                                        triumphantly)

                It's alive! It's alive!
                I've succeeded!

                    VICTOR

                Henry - in the name of God -

CAMERA MOVES SWIFTLY FORWARD
TO HUGE CU FRANKENSTEIN, as
he stands, his feet apart,
arms upstretched, peal after
peal of laughter bursting from
his throat as he screams:

                    FRANKENSTEIN

                In the same of God! Now I
                know how it feels to be God!

                    FADE OUT

SEQUENCE "E"

(SOUND OF FAR-OFF
EERIE HOWLING)

FADE IN:

E-1   EXT. VILLAGE STREET - NIGHT

The street is silent and
deserted. There are no
lights in any of the
windows. The flare of a
solitary street lamp flickers
wanly in the evening wind,
creating a small pool of light
in the surrounding darkness.

A man comes hurrying down the
street, past camera - CAMERA
PICKS HIM UP AND PANS SWIFTLY
WITH HIM until he pauses before a doorway and knocks
hurriedly, as if he could not
stand being alone in that dark,
silent street, with the fear-
some, far-off howling for company.

(SOUND: HOWLING OFF)

While he waits for someone to
open the door, he cocks his
head and listens and seems to
shrink down into his upturned
coat collar - then there is the
faint sound of the drawing of a
bolt and the door is opened
half-way and a white face appears,
like a handkerchief against the
dark, bidding him enter.

He slips inside and we hear the
sound of the bolt being dropped
back into place and

DISSOLVE THROUGH TO:

E-2   EXT. PEASANT'S COTTAGE - NIGHT

A small cottage with a thatched
roof, presumably on the outskirts
of the town. The door is half
open, and peering through into
the darkness outside and listen-   (HOWLING SOUNDS LOUDER)
ing are two old peasants - one,
an old man, with a lantern raised
aloft: the other, a bent old woman
with a pope. They listen, a look
of fright on their faces. CAMERA
MOVES SLOWLY UP TO COUPLE AS
THEY SPEAK

(CONTINUED)

E-2   (CONTINUED)

       OLD MAN
         It sounds like the cry of the
         were-wolf -

       OLD WOMAN

         Ja, some evil thing is abroad.

She crosses herself.
As they draw instinctively
back into the shelter of
the cottage, slowly closing
the door against this un-
known terror.

DISSOLVE THROUGH TO:

E-3 INT. ANOTHER PEASANT COTTAGE -
    NIGHT - CLOSE SHOT AT WINDOW

A young peasant mother, with
a candle in her hand, is listening at the window, the curtain
half drawn aside. Behind her,
is a picturesque cradle, a   (HOWLING STILL LOUDER)
young baby is sleeping. The
young mother drops the curtain
back into place and moves slowly
to a crucifix hanging on the wall
next to the window. Setting the
cradle down upon a carved chest
beneath the crucifix, she sinks
to her knees in silent prayer.

DISSOLVE THROUGH TO:

E-4 EXT. VERY LONG SHOT - HILL -
    NIGHT

A glass or process shot of the
bleak mountains that encompass
the valley. Far up on the   (HOWLING RISING TO
rocky heights is the dark out-   CRESCENDO)
line of the mill. A tiny light
is burning, a mere pin-prick in
the dark.

CAMERA STARTS TO MOVE FORWARD
as we

DISSOLVE THROUGH TO: (HOWLING CUT SHORT
            ABRUPTLY BY THE
            CRACK OF A WHIP)

E-5   INT. CELLAR OF MILL -
      NIGHT - CLOSE SHOT OF
      FRANKENSTEIN'S HAND

   wielding a vicious-looking
   whip, which has just uncoiled,
   like a snake striking, and is
   being withdrawn.

   CAMERA MOVES QUICKLY BACK TO
   FULL SCENE, as Frankenstein
   lashes out again with the whip -
   it hisses through the air and
   cracks again. He is panting
   heavily, and looks harried and
   almost exhausted.

   The interior of the cellar is
   a place of indeterminate size
   with an uneven floor covered with
   dirty straw and debris. Dark
   old beams, sagging a little with
   age, support the roof, The
   stone walls of the cellar are
   damp and covered with fungus.

   In a nearby corner, in the shadow
   of a beam, chained to a ring in
   the wall, the Monster crouches,
   a huddled, formless mass. At
   the foot of three broad steps
   leading up out of the cellar is
   the dwarf, hunched up over a
   small brazier of glowing coals,
   holding in his hand an iron
   poker, the other end of which
   rests in the bed of coals.

                     FRANKENSTEIN
                  (lowering the whip a
                   little breathless)
              Hah - there - ! You've begin-
              ning to understand my language
              eh? No more of that howling -
              the whole countryside will be
              upon us -

   Stands looking down at
   the Monster, regaining
   his breath, trembling
   nervously.

E-6   INT. FLASH CLOSE UP -
      DWARF

   watching, his eyes wide
   with terrified fascination -
   the glow of the coals in the
   brazier lighting his pinched
   features. He grips the hot
   iron tightly, as if his very
   life depended upon keeping a
   firm hold on it.

e-7 int. cellar - wide angle

Frankenstein, as if satisfied that the Monster has been cowed for the time being, drops his whip and addresses the dwarf wearily, with a note of discouragement in his voice.

       FRANKENSTEIN
      Ah. Fritz, Fritz, it's going to
      be no easy task to tame this
      fellow -

CAMERA MOVES FORWARD TO CLOSE UP OF WHIP ON FLOOR and then across towards the Monster. Frankenstein's voice continues, unbroken over scene. Monster's arm comes slowly, stealthily into scene - the white, almost bloodless fingers reaching for the whip as it lies on the floor.

      -He has the strength of ten
      men - until we can reach his
      brain - his reason - and teach
      him, little by little - first
      by fear - then as a child,
      learning one simple lesson at
      at time -

E-8 INT. CELLAR - REVERSE ANGLE

Huge shape of the Monster in immediate fore., as he slowly works his way towards the whip, dragging his heavy chain behind him.

Frankenstein's speech is interrupted by a squeal of alarm from the dwarf, as he observes this furtive movement. Frankenstein whirls around just in time to catch the Monster in the act of picking up the whip. He leaps back with a cry of anger, and fear as the Monster starts to rise on his haunches, dark and menacing, his great form almost blotting out the scene.

Frankenstein stumbles back towards the dwarf, screaming:

       FRANKENSTEIN
      The iron! The iron!

E-9   INT. FLASH CLOSE SHOT -
        BRAZIER

    as the white-hot iron is
    hastily snatched from its
    bed of glowing coals

E-10   INT. CELLAR - WIDE ANGLE

    matching action as dwarf
    passes the hot iron to
    Frankenstein, who draws
    himself up into a masterful
    attitude and advances upon
    the Monster, who still
    dominates the fore., back
    to camera

                    FRANKENSTEIN
                Back! Back! Down!

                        (brandishing poker)

            Fire - fire - !

E-11   INT. FLASH LARGE CLOSE
        UP - WHITE HOT IRON

    lunging swiftly into
    camera as Frankenstein ad-
    vances - white-hot incandescent

E-12   INT. FLASH LARGE CLOSE UP -
        MONSTER'S FACE

    contorted with rage and fear
    as he retreats before the iron,
    snarling.

E-13   INT. WIDE ANGLE

    matching action as Frankenstein
    drives the Monster back into his
    corner - as Monster hesitates
    momentarily, Frankenstein touches
    him with the tip of the poker -
    Monster utters an injured bellow
    and drops to the floor, shrinking
    from the searing contact.

                        (CONTINUED)

E-13   (CONTINUED)

    Frankenstein picks up
    the whip, which the
    Monster has dropped at
    sight of the hot iron,
    and stands over him for
    a moment, furiously.

                    FRANKENSTEIN
                         (making signs)
                Obey me - master - master!
                      (indicating poker)
                Fire - fire - pain -

Monster crouches even
lower, looking up at
Frankenstein with an
expression of dumb animal
hate and fear.

Frankenstein sways a little
dizzily, as if spent with
his exertions.

                    FRANKENSTEIN
                        (holding out iron to dwarf)

                Fritz - here - take this -

Dwarf sidles warily forward,
taking the iron from his
shaking hand, and turns towards
the Monster. Frankenstein
leans weakly back against the
wall, regarding his creation
with horror-stricken eyes.

Dwarf, hovering just out of
the Monster's reach, starts
making quick, bewildering dabs
at it - the Monster snarls.

E-14   INT. FLASH CLOSE UP - DWARF

    his face a grinning mask of impish
    glee, as he poked at the Monster
    with the iron, teasing him.

E-15   INT. FLASH CLOSE UP - MONSTER

    snarling sullenly as the tip
    of the iron flashes in and out
    of scene, threatening but
    never touching him.

E-16   INT. MED. SHOT

Frankenstein in fore -
says sharply:

                    FRANKENSTEIN

                    Stop that, Fritz!

Dwarf ceases, a little
sulkily - withdraws a
foot or two and squats
down on his haunches,
watching the Monster with
an air of imbecilic fas-
cination.

Frankenstein covers his
face with his hands for a
moment, beaten and dis-
couraged - looks miserably
across at the Monster and mumbles:

                    FRANKENSTEIN
                    God help me - it isn't a man -
                    it doesn't reason like a man -
                    it's a beast - a nightmare!
                    Something's gone wrong -

                        (whispering)

                    -something - something - some-
                    thing -

                        (beating his hands together
                         in desperation)

                    Where did I fail - what did I
                    overlook - something - something -
                    it's terrible - horrible -

His voice trails away
brokenly, as he turns
toward the stairs with
the air of a man completely
spent.

Dwarf watches him - Frankenstein,
as if suddenly remembering his
presence, turns and says in
lifeless tones:

                    FRANKENSTEIN

                    Come along - bring the iron -
                    and the fire . . . I can't think -
                    I must have rest - rest

                        (dully)

                    Maybe if I go to sleep and
                    awaken it will be gone -

(CONTINUED)

E-16 (CONTINUED)

Exits tiredly through the door - dwarf gives one final poke at the Monster, who snarls back - then picks up the brazier and scurries after Frankenstein with a single fearful backward glance at the Monster. The door closes behind them, plunging the cellar into comparative darkness and CAMERA PANS SWIFTLY TO MED. CLOSE SHOT MONSTER.

For a moment it lies quiescent, listening, waiting - then, when there are no further sounds, it starts slowly to stir. It crawls slowly to its haunches - then up on all fours - then to its feet, standing erect and shaking its chains furiously. Then it starts to snarl, softly at first, but growing louder and louder - it redoubles its efforts to break loose from the heavy chains, but without success. This increases its rage and it starts lunging violently, its snarls rising to a baffled roar. Bellow after bellow resounds through the darkness as it continues to lunge in all directions, in a desperate but futile effort to break the restraining chains.

FADE OUT

SEQUENCE F

(STREET NOISES)

FADE IN:

F-1 EXT. VILLAGE STREET. DAY
MOVING SHOT

The first thing we see is a
LARGE CLOSEUP of a simple
bouquet of springs flowers,
as held in the chubby hands
of the burgomeister, flat
against his middle, which is
adorned by a fancy waistcoat.
The bouquet bobs slightly
up and down in rhythmic accompaniment to his triumphal progress
along the village street.
CAMERA MOVES ON AHEAD OF BURGO-
MEISTER, revealing him in the
full effulgence of his fancy   (STREET NOISES)
waistcoat, very best suit, and
little green felt hat with a
feather thrust gaily on the
hat-band. As he passes along
the street, bowing and smiling
ceremoniously right and left,
CAMERA KEEPS A LITTLE IN ADVANCE
OF HIM, and we glimpse the every-
day activities of the little
mountain village. A pair of
village girls, simpering and
giggling, pass by and acknowledge
his condescending smile.

              GIRLS
        Good day, Herr Burgomeister -

They turn their heads after
him, giggling around the
flowers....At the curb, a
young Czech, a scissors-
grinder with his little
wheeled stand is sharpening
the household knives of an
amiable looking frau who waits,
with three or four children
glad in the picturesque peasant
costume, frisking at her heals.
She gossips with the young Czech,
pausing absently now and then to

(CONTINUED)

92

F-1　(CONTINUED)

    administer a good-natured slap in the general direction of the more obstreperous of her brood...A mongrel dog slinks by...The burgomeister continues along past the door of the village inn, where five or six convivial souls are lounging with tankards of beer, which the bald, rotund inn-keeper is drawing from a huge keg propped up on it's side at one side of the doorway.

                      GROUP
        Good-day Herr Vogel...
        Where are you going with the
        flowers?...Stop for
        stein, Herr Burgomeister.

    Burgomeister smiles important-ly, replying as he passes by the group:

                      BURGOMEISTER
        I am going to see Baron
        Frankenstein. I must not
        keep him waiting.

    Passes on with a jovial wave of his hand - follow his progress with their eyes impressed.

                      GROUP
        The Baron...It must be
        about the wedding...Ja..

E-2　INT. LIVING ROOM CHALET
     DAY MED. SHOT

    Baron Frankenstein, a tall, distinguished-looking man with iron-grey hair, is facing Victor, who is seated on the piano bench, looking extremely ill at ease. Nearby stands Elizabeth, her face wearing a look of acute distress and reproof. It is evident that Victor's report on Henry Frankenstein has been anything but satisfactory, and that he has just passed through a bad half hour.

    (CONTINUED)

F-2   (CONTINUED)

      ELIZABETH (Protesting)

        But, Victor, you haven't
        told us anything - really -

Victor avoids her eyes, and starts to fiddle absently on the keys of the piano, with one finger. The Baron glares indignantly down at him, his manner suspicious and truculent.

      BARON
        You're holding something back!
        What is it?

Victor continues to poke at the keys.

        Stop that, sir!

Victor stops, but does not raise his eyes. The Baron continues to glare down at him for a moment - then growls:

        Well?

Victor rises wearily and Xes to a nearby table, where he takes a cigarette from a little carved box and says, doggedly:

      VICTOR
        That's all there is to tell.
        Henry's well - very busy -
        and asks me to say that he
        will get in touch with
        you later.

Closes box and moves away from table, lighting cigarette with the air of a man who can be pushed no further.

      BARON (In high dudgeon)

        Ah! So! That is
        his only message to his father!
        And his fiancee! He will get
        in touch with us later! Bah!

Flings himself angrily into a chair.

F-3   INT. LIVING ROOM
      CLOSE SHOT AT DOOR

A maid-servant enters and
stands respectfully by the
half-opened door - looks
from one to the other
and sees that something is
wrong - gulps and says
timidly:

                    MAID-SERVANT

                         Herr Baron -

          BARON (Testily; out of scene)

                         Well? Well? What is it?

                    MAID-SERVANT

                         Herr Vogel, the burgomeister.

                    BARON

                         Show him in! Show him in!

Maid-servant nods
timidly, and swings
door open to full width.
The burgomeister stands
just over the threshold
beaming, expansive, still
clutching his bouquet.

                    BURGOMEISTER   (obsequiously)

                         Good day, Herr Baron.
                              (bowing to Elizabeth)
                         Fraulein -

Advances into the living
room, CAMERA PRECEDING HIM
CAMERA HESITATES, first
picking up Elizabeth - the
burgomeister bows as low
as his girth will permit and
hands her the flowers with a
flourish, saying ceremoniously:

                    BURGOMEISTER

                         For the bride -

Elizabeth takes the flowers,
amused in spite of her harried
frame of mind - smiles and
says gravely:

                    ELIZABETH
                         Thank you, Herr Vogel.

(CONTINUED)

F-3   (CONTINUED)

He bows again, highly pleased with himself, and continues on past her towards the Baron, CAMERA PRECEEDING HIM TO WIDER ANGLE. As he passes by Victor, who has dropped down upon the piano bench again, he acknowledges his presence with a less ceramonious, but still highly deferentic bow.

                BURGOMEISTER
            Ah - Herr Moritz! You are
            making music, ja?

Victor smiles politely, hardly conscious of the man's presence. The burgomeister finds himself facing the Baron's unsmiling face -sees that the Baron is in no mood for pleasantries, and becomes very formal, almost official.

                BURGOMEISTER
            All the village is waiting
            for you to name the wedding
            day, Herr Baron. They have
            been preparing - ach - such
            expectation -

baron stares at him for a moment, frowning as if to collect his thoughts to crystallize them into some sort of a decision - then says, rising with a suddenly positive air:

                BARON
            The wedding will take place
            three weeks from tomorrow.

Victor and Elizabeth glance quickly at him - Elizabeth with an air of unspoken protest which dies, still-born, on her lips - Victor with a helpless shrug, as if he were powerless to do any more than he has. Baron looks from one to the other as if challenging them to contradict him - they both turn away. The burgomeister is greatly pleased.

(CONTINUED)

F-3   (CONTINUED - 2)

                       BURGOMEISTER

> Ah - good - good! It will be a gala occasion - a fete day -
>   (gaily, to Victor)
> And you, Herr Moritz - the best man, ja?
>   (rattling on enthusiatically)
> And such a lovely bride - such a fine young man - Herr Frankenstein - so like his father - we are proud -
>   (hastily apologetically, as he catches the Baron's eye)
> I must go - I have duties

Starts to back off towards the door, bowing to each of them in turn, hoping he hasn't said too much or stayed too long.

                     BURGOMEISTER

> Good day, Herr Baron . . .
> Good day, fraulein . . .
> Herr Moritz . . .

Backs out of the door, which the maid-servant has obligingly held open for him. She follows him out, shutting off his farewells by closing the door behind her. The Baron addresses Elizabeth and Victor with an air of savage conclusiveness.

                     BARON

> There - you see? Everything in readiness! Henry must come home! I'll wait for none of his impudent messages - I'll go fetch him myself - tomorrow -
>   (starts toward the door)

VICTOR   (quickly)

Baron pauses belligerently.   No, no -
Elizabeth regards Victor
sadly, positive that he is
concealing something by
his unwitting display of
anxiety

                     BARON

> And why not, sir?

F-3   (CONTINUED - 3)

    Victor looks thoroughly
    miserable - would like to
    tell them the whole horrible
    truth, but doesn't dare -
    he looks towards Elizabeth for
    support, but encounters only
    her look of grave reproof,
    of disappointment in him.
    The Baron continues to eye
    Victor in high displeasure -
    Victor finally mumbles:

                      VICTOR

                  Why - his work -

              BARON   (Interrupting harshly)

                  Bah! His wedding - that is
                  what really matters! I want
                  him here - I shall bring him
                  here - Xes towards the door,

    where he pauses for a
    moment, his hand on the
    door-knob, to repeat,
    emphatically:

                  Tomorrow!

    Exits, slamming the door
    behind him.

    Victor and Elizabeth are
    left alone. For a moment
    they face each other,
    Victor unhappy, not knowing
    what to say, dreading any
    further discussion of the
    terrible secret which he dare
    not disclose - Elizabeth,
    her reproach more marked than
    ever. She Xes to him, plead-
    ingly, and lays her hand on
    his arm, saying in lowered
    tones:

                      ELIZABETH

                  Victor - there is
                  something else - you
                  can tell me -

    He just looks at her
    without replying.
    She tries again, her
    mind groping for the more
    obvious solutions to the
    riddle.

                  Has he - is there - some
                  other woman he has met?

              VICTOR   (sharply)
                  No!

F-3   (CONTINUED - 4)

>Her eyes search his face
>imploringly for some
>sign of his relenting, but
>he only turns away. Not
>to be putt off this time, she
>takes his face between her
>hands and turns it back so
>that he must look directly
>into her eyes.

                    ELIZABETH   (gently)

                        Please -

>He remains sympathetic but
>firm - then, moved by a
>sudden impulse, he removes
>her hands and holding them
>tightly in his, blurts out:

                    VICTOR

                        Elizabeth - I -

>Then he stops and, releas-
>ing her hands, shakes his
>head and moves slowly away
>from her side, saying with
>a resigned shrug:

                        No - there's no use -

>Xes to table and picks up his
>hat, staring down at it as if
>it were some unfamiliar object -
>it is obvious that this is
>probably the hardest thing he
>has ever had to do in all his
>life, that it is a situation
>his ordinary resources cannot
>cope with. Elizabeth, real-
>izing defeat, gives him a long
>look - then she shrugs hope-
>lessly and Xes towards terrace.
>Victor watches her as she steps
>through the low window out
>into the sunshine. Then he
>sighs deeply and stands star-
>int down at his hat, turning
>it over and over in his hands,
>not knowing what to say or do -
>not wanting to leave like this.
>Finally, he replaces the hat on
>the table and starts slowly
>after Elizabeth, as if something
>further had occurred to him,
>something he must ask her.
>CAMERA FOLLOWS HIM THROUGH

(CONTINUED)

F-3   (CONTINUED - 5)

WINDOW TO MED CLOSE SHOT
ON TERRACE

Elizabeth glances around hopefully as she hears him come up behind her, but her faintly-revived hopes are short-lived as she sees that he has no intention of revealing any more than before. It is something else this time. She waits for him to speak. He fumbles awkwardly for a moment, and then says slowly, uncertainly:

       VICTOR

        Elizabeth - what would
        happen if - how would you
        feel in case -

Pauses, as if hardly daring to be presumptuous enough to even frame his question.

        What I'm getting at is: how
        much do you love Henry?

She appears puzzled, and does not answer at once. When she does, she avoids his direct gaze.

       ELIZABETH (in low tones)

        That's a strange question,
        Victor - from you -

       VICTOR   (still groping)

        Henry's father seems to be
        more concerned about this
        wedding than you -

       ELIZABETH

        Victor!

       VICTOR   (shame facedly)

        Well -
         (his voice trails off
         unhappily)

       ELIZABETH

        Baron Frankenstein was my
        father's dearest friend -
        it was all arranged when
        Henry and I were children -

Victor nods grimly, as if her words confirmed some secret conviction of his own. Then he seizes

(CONTINUED)

F-3 (CONTINUED - 6)

her unexpectedly by
the shoulders, and look-
ing deeply into her troubled
eyes, asks almost fiercely:

                  VICTOR
                        Elizabeth - tell me - truly!
                        You really love him, don't you?

                  ELIZABETH   (without much con-
                                  viction)
                        Yes - of course -
                              (as if to settle a
                              doubt in her own mind)
                        And he loves me -

            VICTOR

                  More than anyone in the world!

            ELIZABETH   (simply)

                  And I am going to marry him.

She and Victor stand very
quietly looking into each
other's eyes, her statement
obviously intended to put
at rest forever any linger-
ing doubts he may have. Then
Victor's arms drop to his
sides and he says in his most
matter-of-fact voice:

            VICTOR

                  Oh course.

He lowers his eyes as he
reaches for his cigarette
case and takes out a cigarette - she turns away and
stands, her chin tilted
with a half-defiant air,
gazing out over the sparkling
waters of the lake. Victor
lights his cigarette with a
consciously firm air, squaring
his shoulders a little - then
he puts the case away and
stands by her side - both of
them quite erect, as if bracing
themselves against something
fortifying themselves against
the unspoken but definite fear
of breaking faith with themselves.

(CONTINUED)

F-3   (CONTINUED - 7)

As they stand there, very
unhappy, very perplexed
but very brave, looking out
at the lake, CAMERA SWINGS UP
OVER THEIR HEADS TO L.S. LAKE
AFTERNOON SKY - a very lovely
shot of a soft, fleecy cloud-
bank, bright in the reflected
rays of the late sun. Then
CAMERA STARTS PANNING SWIFTLY
as we:

DISSOLVE THROUGH TO:

SEQUENCE "G"

G-1 EXT. FLASH L.S. LATE AFTERNOON SKY

as CAMERA PANS into mass of dark, threatening clouds which become denser with movement of camera.

DISSOLVE THROUGH TO

G-2 INT. LABORATORY IN TOWER. DAY.

Shooting from floor towards Dr. Waldman, who is seated on the sofa in an attitude of profound thought. Frankenstein is pacing up and down into camera and away - disheveled and almost frantic. From the quavering of his voice - the quick, nervous gesticulations of his hands - the spasmodic jerking of his head, it is evident that he has almost reached the breaking point.

>   FRANKENSTEIN
>   I don't know what to do -
>   which way to turn! It's
>   become a nightmare - an
>   obsession that haunts me
>   day and night!

G-3 INT. CU WALDMAN

following Frankenstein's movement with his eyes - says gravely:

>   WALDMAN
>   What if he should break
>   loose and escape.

G-4 INT. CU FRANKENSTEIN

pausing with a hunted look.

>   FRANKENSTEIN
>   I don't dare even think of
>   such a thing!

G-5 INT. MED. SHOT

Waldman in fore. - he rises and regards the distracted man before him with stern eyes.

G-5 (CONTINUED)

      WALDMAN

    But you Must thin of it!
    That creature - with the
    brain you stole - the brain
    of a vicious and brutal killer ▯

      FRANKENTEIN

    Stop! I haven't had a moment's
    peace since you first told me!

Walks away from Waldman, over
to work-table, covering his face
with his hands. Waldman follows
him - CAMERA PANS INTO C.S,
AT WORK TABLE.

      WALDMAN (earnestly)
    It's a menace to mankind! It
    should be destroyed!

Frankenstein raises harried eyes
to his.

      FRANKENSTEIN

    Destroy my life work? Destroy
    the greatest achievement in
    the history of medical science?

      WALDMAN   (insistently)
    An achievement if you like - yes!
    But not great, because it is not
    perfect! It is a monstrosity -
    only evil can come!

      FRANKENSTEIN

    But it's somehow part of me -
    linked to me - !
      (with a gesture of despair)
    Oh, what good are words, now?
    I'm being punished - punished!
    I tried to make myself God's
    equal - this is His answer

As he says this, in tones of
dejected self-condemnation, from
the lower part of the tower comes
a sudden scream. They both stiffen
listening   MAN'S SCREAM

      WALDMAN

    What!

      FRANKENSTEIN

    Fritz - !

(CONTINUED)

G-5   CONTINUED

    Turns and rushes across the
    room, flinging open door lead-
    ing to main part of tower - Wald-
    man hurries after him, CAMERA
    PANNING SWIFTLY

G-6   INT. TOWER MEDIUM SHOT TOP
      OF STAIRS

    shooting up from angle a few feet
    below. Another scream sounds from   (SOUND OF SCREAM)
    direction of cellar. Fainter than
    the first. Frankenstein and Waldman
    come running out of the laboratory
    and start down the stairs, CAMERA
    SPIRALLING SWIFTLY TO FOLLOW.

    DISSOLVE THROUGH TO

g-7   INT. lower floor of tower
      MED. SHOT AT FOOT OF STAIRS

    As Frankenstein and Waldman reach
    the bottom of the stairs and hurry
    across to small door leading to
    the cellar, CAMERA PANNING TO
    FOLLOW. Frankenstein snatches
    up his whip, which is hanging
    from a peg at one side of the
    door, and pushes open the door.
    CAMERA MOVES QUICKLY FORWARD TO
    CLOSE SHOT AT DOOR as they
    pause, transfixed wit horror
    at what they see.

G-8   INT. WIDE ANGLE CELLAR

    as seen from doorway. Silhouetted
    against the far wall is the shadow
    of the dwarf, hanging by the neck
    from a low beam, his limp body
    swaying silently to and fro. From
    the darkness that enfolds the
    rest of the room there is the
    sound of a low snarl and the huge
    black form of the Monster hurls
    itself into camera.

G-9   INT CELLAR.
      FLASH CLOSE SHOT AT DOOR

    Frankenstein and Waldman looking
    in aghast - Frankenstein grabs
    Waldman and yanks him back, shouting

                      FRANKENSTEIN
                      Look out!

(CONTINUED)

G-9   (CONTINUED)

    Slams the door just as the Monster throws himself furiously against it, escaping just in the nick of time. Monster starts lunging against the door, howling.

G-10   INT. LOWER FLOOR OF TOWER.
        MED CLOSE SHOT AT CELLAR DOOR,

    as Frankenstein hastily drops the bolt into place, securing the door for the time being. From the other side, the Monster's terrific onslaughts cause the oaken panels to quiver. Safe for the moment, Frankenstein totters away and leans weakly against the wall, trembling violently, completely unnerved.

> FRANKENSTEIN
>
> Oh - oh -!
>
> WALDMAN (sharply)
>
> Come, come - get hold of yourself!
>
> FRANKENSTEIN
>
> He hated Fritz - Fritz has been teasing him - I tried to make him stop.
> (Drops Whip)

Waldman regards him grimly, glancing back over his shoulder towards the bolted door - then says, in incisive tones

> WALDMAN
>
> Now is there any doubt in your mind about what should be done with your infernal creation?
>
> FRANKENSTEIN
>
> What can we do?

Xes wearily to stairs and drops down upon the bottom step, his face drawn and ghastly with the memory of the horror he has seen and the horror yet to come. CAMERA MOVES INTO CLOSE SHOT as Waldman joins him, continuing:

G-10   CONTINUED

> WALDMAN
>> We must kill it - like any savage animal that's had its first taste of human blood!
>
> FRANKENSTEIN
>> Murder   (recoiling)
>> Murder - !
>
> WALDMAN
>> Is it murder to kill a mad dog? Listen to that -

G-11   INT. FLASH CU DOOR,
as the Monster within continues crashing against it, howling and snarling.

G-12   INT. MED CLOSE SHOT

matching action as Waldman points. They both listen, Waldman going on:

> WALDMAN
>> Your Monster is more dangerous than a hundred mad dogs!
>>   (as Frankenstein looks up at him dazedly)
>> We can do it scientifically - painlessly.
>
> FRANKENSTEIN
>> How?
>
> WALDMAN   (thinking fast)
>> Wait - it will come to me -

He stares intently at Frankenstein for a moment, with unseeing eyes, deep in thought - then says:

>> Have you morphia? A hypodermic syringe?

frankenstein nods - glances toward door incredulously as he says:

> frankenstein
>> Yes - but surely you're not going to try to make an injection now - !

From out of scene comes the crashing sound of another fierce onslaught on the door.   (SOUND OF MONSTER BATTERING)

G-12 (CONTINUED)

>   WALDMAN
>
>   We can trick him, We have brains -
>   (As Frankenstein continues
>   to regard him incredulously)
>   Ah, yes, I know there is a risk -
>   a great risk, but . . . a quarter
>   grain solution - what they call
>   they hypnotic dose. . . it will make
>   him unconscious for hours - then we
>   can decide what to do - the best
>   way to -
>   (Breaking off sharply)
>   Quick! Go fetch the drug!

Frankenstein gets slowly and unwillingly to his feet, anything but convinced that this is the thing to do.

>   FRANKENSTEIN
>
>   But how -
>
>   WALDMAN (with fierce impatience)
>
>   In another few minutes he'll be
>   through that door!

He swings Frankenstein around and starts to push him up the stairs, exclaiming:

>   It's our one chance!

Frankenstein disappears up the stairs, a little faster now, as if spurred on by a sudden realization that Waldman is right. Waldman turns back towards door, CAMERA MOVING BACK TO WIDER ANGLE WITH DOOR IN FORE. - Monster is still trying to break through. Blow after blow cause the stout panel to tremble and crack. Waldman tense - nervous approaches the door gingerly and stands watching and listening - then moves alertly about, as if planning what to do.

G-13 INT. LABORATORY
shooting towards door in b.g. In immediate fore. is a glass cabinet, of the type used in surgeon' offices, containing bottles of drugs and various solutions, surgical instruments, small, delicate bits of apparatus, etc. Frankenstein hurries in from door and rushes over to cabinet in fore. - pulls down bottle containing drug and a hypodermic outfit.

G-14   CELLAR
        FLASH CLOSE SHOT OF MONSTER

    hurling himself against the door,
    which has commenced to show
    signs of giving way.

G-15   INT. MED SHOT LOWER FLOOR

    Waldman moving about with quick,
    worried steps - Xes to well of
    stairs and shouts up:

                    WALDMAN

                Hurry! Hurry!

G-16   INT. TOP OF STAIRS.

    Frankenstein, with hypodermic
    outfit in his hand comes running
    out of laboratory and down the
    stairs.

G-17   INT. MED. SHOT LOWER FLOOR.

    Waldman waiting anxiously at
    bottom of stairs - Frankenstein
    comes down - thrusts the
    outfit at Waldman, saying
    breathlessly:

                    FRANKENSTEIN

                What are you going to do now?

                    WALDMAN
                        (grimly)
                Open the door!

G-18   INT. FLASH CU FRANKENSTEIN,
        gasping

                    FRANKENSTEIN

                What!

G-19   INT. MED. SHOT ANOTHER ANGLE
        Matching action as Frankenstein
        stares at Waldman in distress
        and makes a move toward Waldman as
        if suspecting his sanity and
        trying to prevent any such
        rash action. Waldman checks
        him with an upraised hand:

                    WALDMAN
                I will stand behind the door
                and as he starts toward you,
                step quickly up behind it
                and - so -
                    (Presses plunger of hypodermic
                    needle by way of illustration)

G-19 (CONTINUED)

>Frankenstein stands staring at him in silence for a moment, weighing the potentialities of this maneuver - then picks up the whip and says crisply:

FRANKENSTEIN

>Very well - I'm ready -

>They both cross to cellar door - CAMERA PANNING TO FOLLOW - Waldman, hypodermic in hand, takes up his post so that he will be concealed behind the door, which opens outward. The assaults on the door have resulted in the stout oaken panel commencing to splinter down the middle. Frankenstein, grasping his whip firmly and preparing to leap back, takes hold of the bolt.

G-20 INT FLASH CLOSE SHOT

>bolt being slowly lifted.

G-21 INT. FLASH CU WALDMAN

>tense, ready to spring.

G-22 INT. CLOSE SHOT FRANKENSTEIN AT DOOR

>matching action as he slips the bolt out of place and leaps quickly back out of scene. As he does so, the door flies open with a crash, and in the doorway stands the Monster, panting glaring into camera.

G-23 INT. FLASH CU FRANKENSTEIN

>uncoiling his whip in Monster's direction with a sharp crack.   (CRACK OF WHIP)

G-24 INT. FLASH LARGE CU WALDMAN

>flat against the wall behind door, every nerve on the qui vive, awaiting his first chance to spring into action.

G-25 LARGE CU MONSTER,
>baring his teeth in a savage snarl as he starts quickly forward into camera. The whip cracks again. Frankenstein's voice comes over CU: (CRACK OF WHIP)

>(Continued)

G-25   (CONTINUED)

                   FRANKENSTEIN

                  Back! Back!

G-26   INT. WIDE ANGLE

    matching action as Monster lunges toward Frankenstein, who falls back, flourishing his whip. The instant the Monster's huge bulk has cleared the doorway, Waldman darts out from his place of concealment and slips behind the Monster. We see him make a quick move - the Monster gives a sudden bellow of pain and wheels - Waldman ducks, but not quite soon enough. A blow from the Monster's hand sends him spinning to the floor.

G-27   INT. FLASH CU FRANKENSTEIN

    starting forward, crying:

                 FRANKENSTEIN
                 Waldman!

G-28   INT. FLASH CU WALDMAN

    lying in a crumpled heap on the floor, very still

G-29   INT. FLASH CU MONSTER

    turning into camera - over his face comes an odd, rather perplexed look - his eyes glaze - he reels slightly

G-30   INT. FLASH OF FRANKENSTEIN
    backing warily along the wall, never one taking his eyes from the Monster's face.

G-31   INT. WIDE ANGLE

    The Monster sways dizzily - makes a final, ineffectual lunge at Frankenstein, and then goes crashing headlong to the floor, unconscious. Frankenstein hesitates but briefly, watching to see if the Monster is really out - then springs to Waldman's side, exclaiming:

                 FRANKENSTEIN

                 Waldman! Are **you** hurt?

G-32   INT. FLASH CU WALDMAN,

    raising himself from the floor
    with a little smile - shakes
    his head.

                      WALDMAN

                          No -

G-33   INT MED. SHOT

    matching action of Waldman gets
    up, calmly brushing himself off.

                      WALDMAN   (dryly)

                          I thought it best to lie
                          quite still -

Frankenstein leans back against the
wall, laughing with slightly hysterical
relief. They both turn and look
down at the Monster. Before either
can speak, Victor appears in the
doorway, pausing breathless. He has
been running.

G-34   INT. FLASH OF VICTOR

    as he starts excitedly forward
    into camera.

                      VICTOR

                          Henry! What's happened?

G-35   INT. WIDE ANGLE

    matching action as Frankenstein
    and Waldman turn at the sound of
    his voice, Frankenstein unpleasantly
    surprised.

                      FRANKENSTEIN

                          Victor! What are **you** doing here?

                    VICTOR
                      You father - Elizabeth - coming
                      up the hill -

G-36   INT. FLASH CU FRANKENSTEIN

    appalled, gasping:

                      FRANKENSTEIN

                          Elizabeth!

G-37   INT. MED SHOT

>matching action as Victor nods
>explaining rapidly:

VICTOR

>I went on ahead - told them
>I'd see if you were here

FRANKENSTEIN
>(desperately)
>Stop them!   Stop them!

Victor Xes swiftly to door and
peers out down the hill

VICTOR

>Too late - here they come -

WALDMAN
>(Indicating body of Monster)
>They mustn't see that!

FRANKENSTEIN

>Hide it! Hurry! Back in the
>cellar -

Waldman starts to
obey - Frankenstein leaps
feverishly to help him. Victor
pulls him away.

VICTOR

>I'll do that! You get up and
>make yourself presentable - you
>look all in -

FRANKENSTEIN (Chokingly)

>I am - terrible thing - Fritz -

WALDMAN

>Strangled -

VICTOR

>My God!
>(muffled "God" as he claps
>his hand to his mouth in
>horror - to Frankenstein
>pointing to doorway.

>Go on - don't stand there - I'll
>keep them down here.

Frankenstein staggers over towards
stairs.

FRANKENSTEIN

>Elizabeth - here - at a time
>like this   (continued)

113

G-37   (CONTINUED)

Gets up weakly just about ready to collapse, leaning against side wall for support. Victor and Waldman start to lug the body of the monster back into the cellar.

                    VICTOR
              Quick - quick -

G-38   INT. TOP OF STAIRS

Frankenstein arrives at top of stairs and lurches in through laboratory door.

G-39   INT. FLASH LOWER FLOOR.

Waldman and Victor moving monster's body toward cellar.

G-40   EXT. WATCH TOWER

The Baron and Elizabeth arrive at top of hill - Baron puffing - he pauses to mop his brow and stare up at the tower with a truculent eye - Elizabeth also looking around curiously, with a little shiver.

                    BARON
              Queer sort of a place for
              Henry to be, I must say!

                    ELIZABETH
              Oh, I hope he's all right -

G-41   INT LOWER FLOOR TOWER
       WIDE ANGLE

In b.g. Waldman has just dragged Monster's body through cellar door - Victor, breathless and a bit disheveled from his exertion, is just closing the door upon Waldman and Monster as Baron and Elizabeth enter in fore.

                    BARON
              Well, Victor - !

Victor wheels forcing a wan smile says inanely:

                    VICTOR

              Oh - Baron -

                    BARON
              (As Victor comes forward)

              Where's Henry?

G-41   (CONTINUED)

                    VICTOR

                         Upstairs in his laboratory.

                    ELIZABETH

                         Is he - all right - ?

                    VICTOR

                         Of course!

Baron regards Victor with
considerable suspicion, noting
his lack of breath, the rumpled
condition of his attire.

                    BARON

                              What's the matter with you?
                              What have you been doing?

                    VICTOR

                         Nothing - I -

                    BARON
                              (with a grunt, turning to
                              stairs)
                         We'll go up. Come Elizabeth.

Victor clutches him hastily by
the arm, deterring him.

                    VICTOR

                              No - if you don't mind - I
                                   (As Baron eyes him
                                   with a frown)
                              I'll go and tell him you're here.
                              He - Henry's very particular
                              about admitting anyone to his
                              laboratory -

                    BARON

                         I'll soon settle this on my own.

                    VICTOR

                         Please - please - let me go -
                         I'll bring him down directly.

                    ELIZABETH

                         Please, Victor - please -

Victor starts hastily up the
stairs. Baron watches him go
with considerable displeasure

G-41   (CONTINUED)

                    BARON
                            Our reception here seems a
                            bit unusual.

                    VICTOR
                            Not at all - I - we'll be
                            right down - right away -

Disappears up the stairs.
Baron turns to Elizabeth with
a disgusted grunt.

                    BARON
                            Well, This does seem to
                            mysterious and Victor's
                            behavior!

                    ELIZABETH
                            Oh, I have a feeling that
                            there's something terribly
                            wrong - (glancing around with
                            a shiver)
                            Such a gloomy old tower
                                (voice trails off vaguely)

G-42   INT. MED. SHOT LABORATORY

Shooting towards door. Frankenstein
lying in a heap on sofa. -Victor
hurries in and Xes anxiously to him.

                    VICTOR
                            Henry - Henry - you are ill!

                    FRANKENSTEIN
                            I can't face them - I can't!
                            It's all too horrible - I'm
                            going out of my mind.

G-43   INT. LOWER FLOOR. WIDE ANGLE
Cellar door in fore. Baron poking
around curiously, making vague
sounds of displeasure in the back
of his throat - Elizabeth stands
at foot of stairs, glancing
anxiously aloft, her hands
tightly clasped, waiting. Suddenly
cellar door in fore. opens and
Waldman backs out, his clothing
disarranged - stands looking
back into cellar and shaking
his head, lips pursed grimly.
Baron and Elizabeth turn and
stare at him. He closes the door
slowly - then turns and sees them
for the first time.

116

G-43 (CONTINUED)

               WALDMAN
                  (apologetically)
                  AH - your Pardon -

Starts toward them CAMERA
FOLLOWING INTO MED. SHOT

                  I'm Doctor Waldman from the
                  University of Goldstadt.

               BARON
                  (with a curt bow)
                  I've heard of you - Doctor. I'm
                  Baron Frankenstein, Henry's
                  father -
                  (Indicates Elizabeth)
                  -and this is Fraulein Elizabeth
                  his betrothed.

Waldman acknowledges the intro-
ductions with grave punctilio -
Elizabeth smiles briefly, her
thoughts elsewhere.
Then the Baron, clearing his
throat testily says:

               BARON

                  Perhaps Doctor you can explain
                  the unexplainable absence of
                  my son -

indicates room with a half
contemptuous flick of his
hand - stands waiting, very
much the Baron. Waldman hesitates, regarding them. Both with the
utmost gravity. Elizabeth's eyes
are filled with anxiety, his very
attitude confirming her
intuitive suspicions. Finally
Waldman says slowly:

               WALDMAN

                  I don't wish to alarm you,
                  Baron Frankenstein - but if you
                  have any regard for your son's
                  sanity, you will take him away
                  at once.

Elizabeth utters a little
cry - Baron places a gently
restraining hand on her arm and
replies:

               BARON

                  I don't quite understand.

(Continued)

G-43   (CONTINUED)

                        WALDMAN
                    When you hear what I have to
                    tell you, you'll probably
                    doubt my own sanity.

                        BARON
                    Please allow me to be the
                    judge of that -

Waldman nods slowly, several
times, trying to decide upon the
best course of action - then he
draws a deep breath and, turning
towards cellar door, says:

                        WALDMAN
                    If you will come with me -

Starts into camera towards cellar
door. Waldman stops, turns and
politely points to Elizabeth.

                    You'll forgive me, but I do
                    not think it wise for the
                    young lady to accompany
                    us any further.

Hesitates significantly.
Elizabeth is commencing to   BARON
be really alarmed by his
constrained manner.   Wait here, my dear

                        WALDMAN
                    It is really best, I believe
                    fraulein.
                        (to Baron)
                    If you will come, Baron -

Both men X to cellar door,
CAMERA MOVING BACK TO CLOSE SHOT
AT DOOR. Here Waldman opens the
door half-way and stands aside
for the Baron to enter - then
follows quickly. As the Baron
steps over the threshold, he
utters a gasp of horror, which
is smothered by the abrupt
closing of the door behind them
both. CAMERA REMAINS ON
CLOSE SHOT DOOR for a few feet.

G-44   INT. FLASH ON ELIZABETH,

        staring, frightened, at the closed
        door.

G-45   INT. MED. SHOT LABORATORY.

Victor assisting Frankenstein to let into some fresh linen and make himself otherwise presentable. Frankenstein has changed from his chemical-stained laboratory clothes to dark trousers and a clean white shirt. He is weak and groggy - leans against end of sofa as Victor approaches him with a stiff drink.

          FRANKENSTEIN

          I can't - I can't - I don't
          want them to see me this
          way -

          VICTOR
              (deliberately, matter-of-fact)
          Here - take this. You'll feel
          more like yourself -

Hands him the drink - Frankenstein sips part of it and then pushes it away. Victor shoves it back at him insisting.

          All of it - it'll give you
          strength -

          FRANKENSTEIN

          Strength - strength -
              (starts laughing crazily)
         - strength!

Dashes the glass to the floor wand starts reeling around the room alternately laughing and crying, careening against whatever appears in his path - Victor frantically trying to hush him.

          VICTOR

          Sh-h-h! Sh-h-h! They'll
          hear you. You'll frighten
          Elizabeth!

          FRANKENSTEIN
              (laughing loudly)
          I won't frighten her, but I
          know something that will! Take
          her down and show her Fritz! Show
          her my masterpiece - go ahead!

G-46   INT. LOWER ROOM
        CLOSE SHOT BOTTOM OF STAIRS.
        Elizabeth looking up - hears
        Frankenstein's wild laughter
        and the sound of falling objects
        from the laboratory above - no
        longer able to stand the
        suspense, she starts running
        up the stairs.

G-47   INT. MED. SHOT CELLAR

        Baron and Waldman in foreground
        looking down at the inert form of the
        monster - in this shot we do not
        see Fritz's body. Waldman has
        evidently just finished telling
        the Baron about the Monster - Baron
        is staggered - speaks in an
        awed whisper.

                        BARON
                I've seen it - and yet I still
                can't believe it - such things
                are against the law of Nature -

                        WALDMAN
                    (pointing simply to monster)

                There is the living proof.

        Baron turns and looks dazedly
        at Waldman - shakes his head
        blankly and looks down at the
        monster again - then raises his
        eyes and looks across the cellar.

G-48   INT CELLAR
        FLASH CU WALL

        the silhouette of Fritz's body
        dangling in shadow on the wall.

G-49   INT. MED. SHOT

        shooting towards door - matching
        action as Baron shudders and turns
        to leave, passing his hand over
        his eyes - says dazedly.

                        BARON
                Take me - to my son -

        Waldman nods in silent acquiescence
        deeply, sympathetic - Baron stumbles
        a little blindly towards door, almost
        feeling his way out. For a moment
        Waldman hesitates looking compas-
        sionately down at the Monster.

G-50   INT. FLASH LARGE CU MONSTER'S FACE

   In spite of its grotesque appearance
   it wears an expression of almost
   human calm.

G-51   INT. CU WALDMAN
   looking down and shaking his head -
   says very softly:

                    WALDMAN

              Poor devil - Poor devil

G-52   INT. MED SHOT CELLAR

   matching action
   as Waldman turns soberly away from
   his compassionate scrutiny of the
   Monster to join the Baron, who
   is watching with terrible fascination,
   unable to tear his eyes away from the
   fantastic spectacle. Baron pushes
   open the door - they start slowly
   out.

G-53   INT WIDE ANGLE LABORATORY

   Frankenstein and Victor in B.g. -
   Frankenstein still laughing, Victor
   trying to quiet him - Elizabeth arrives,
   out of breath, in doorway in fore.-
   call uncertainly:

                    ELIZABETH

                  Henry -

G-54   FLASH OF FRANKENSTEIN,

   whirling into camera - the wild
   laughter dies from his lips as
   he sees Elizabeth -
   he makes a tremendous effort to
   pull himself together.

G-55   INT. CU ELIZABETH

   standing in doorway with a
   tender, half-dubious smile - she
   holds out her arms to him
   saying softly:

                    ELIZABETH

                  Henry - my dear -

G-56   MED. CLOSE SHOT FRANKENSTEIN

    as he starts towards Elizabeth - on
    her face is a curious, almost
    childish, look of uncertainty
    he seems to be struggling for enough
    strength to reach the haven of her arms.

G-57   INT. WIDE ANGLE LABORATORY

    matching action as Elizabeth and
    Frankenstein X towards each other.
    Victor stands watching in sympathetic
    silence. From across the width of
    the room Frankenstein is advancing
    slowly falteringly, the same
    curious look on his face. As they
    approach each other, in fore. Frank-
    enstein cries piteously:

                  FRANKENSTEIN

                  Elizabeth - !

    and collapses at her feet. She
    drops to her knees beside him.
    Victor, who has already sprung
    forward:

                  ELIZABETH
                  Victor! Quick!

    Victor snatches up another glass
    and pours it half-full of liquor -
    hurries into fore., where Elizabeth
    is on her knees with Frankenstein's
    head in her arms, exclaiming:

                  Oh my dear, my dear -
                  what have they done to you?

    Victor gives her the glass - together
    they start to force drink down Frank-
    enstein's throat. Elizabeth says:

                  Call the Baron!

    Victor rises and hurries out.

G-58   INT. LOWER FLOOR TOWER

    Baron and Waldman emerging slowly
    from the cellar - Baron still like a
    man in a trance. As Waldman closes
    the cellar door behind them, the
    voice of Victor cuts in sharply from
    above.

                  VICTOR'S VOICE

                  Baron! Doctor Waldman!
                  Come quickly

G-58   (CONTINUED)

    This brings the Baron from his
    daze with a jerk - he and Waldman
    X to stairs and start up on the
    run.

G-59   INT. LABORATORY WIDE ANGLE

    as Victor comes back into the
    room - Elizabeth is seated on the
    floor, Frankenstein's head cradled
    in her arms - she is rocking him
    back and forth like a child - casts
    an appealing glance at Victor, who
    answers her mute inquiry with a
    terse:

                VICTOR

              They're coming -

                ELIZABETH
                      (almost frantic with anxiety)
              Victor, he's ill - he's very ill!
              We must take him away - take him
              home today -

As she says this, the Baron and
Waldman enter hastily.

                BARON   (rushing foreward)

              What's happening? What's the
              matter with him?

                VICTOR

              He fainted -

                BARON

              Get him up on that sofa!

Elizabeth rises - Baron and
Victor pick Frankenstein up
and carry him over to sofa -
CAMERA MOVING OVER TO CLOSE
SHOT
Baron pushes everybody aside and
sits down of sofa beside Frankenstein,
chafing his hands, barking out orders
greatly concerned and still considerably
shaken by the events of the past few
minutes. Waldman hovers about behind sofa -
Elizabeth stands at Baron's shoulder
Victor picks up glass of liquor
and holds it out for Baron to
administer.

G-59   (CONTINUED)

                        BARON
                            (to the others)
                    Here - get away - let me sit
                    there -
                            (To Frankenstein)
                    Henry - Henry! Open your eyes
                    I'm here - your father -

                            (taking glass from Victor)
                    Give me that!
                            (forces liquor between
                            Frankenstein's lips.

                    There - there - that's better -
                    He'll come around
                            (glaring at Waldman)
                    So this is what happens to
                    students at your University!

                        WALDMAN
                            (smiling with gentle tolerance)
                    It is none of my doing - you will
                    learn all about it in time -

G-60   INT. FLASH OF FRANKENSTEIN

Commencing to come around - rolls
his head weakly from side to side.
Baron's hand into scene, feeding
him more liquor - his
voice saying crisply:

                        BARON

                    He's better now. We're going
                    home with him at once!

Frankenstein opens his eyes - tries
to shake his head, moaning.

                        FRANKENSTEIN

                    No - no - my work

G-61   INT. CLOSE SHOT BOTH

matching motion as Frankenstein speaks.
Baron replies truculently:

                        BARON

                    You work eh? You forget
                    about your work for while.

                        FRANKENSTEIN

                    All my labors - useless -
                    lost forever -

G-61 (CONTINUED)

    Waldman comes around from back of
    sofa - touches Baron gently on the
    arm - says gently:

                      WALDMAN

                      Permit me -

    baron looking up - rises - Waldman
    take his place - clasps Frankenstein's
    hand soothingly in his and says with
    a reassuring smile.

                      You must not worry -
                      Everything will be taken
                      care of - scientifically
                      -Everything -

                      FRANKENSTEIN
                      What will happen to my work
                      the notes - my experiments

                      WALDMAN

                      I'll see that they are
                      preserved - and they are
                      saved. You will write them into
                      a book - for the world to read -
                      and try to understand.

                      FRANKENSTEIN

                      Yes - yes -
                          (looks past Waldman at
                            Elizabeth)
                      Elizabeth -

    Waldman rises - Elizabeth drops down
    upon the sofa beside Frankenstein - takes
    him in her arms - the others turn away
    as we

                    DISSOLVE THROUGH TO

SEQUENCE "H"

H-1 EXT L.S. GARDENS AT CHALET AFTERNOON   (STAGE OF BACKLOT LAKE)

A sloping rock garden descends to the shores of the lake at one side of the chalet, which is in the b.g. - very charming, picturesque angle. Frankenstein and Elizabeth are strolling towards camera. His appearance is radically changed since the preceeding sequence - he looks rested and happier, normal again. Elizabeth is grave and thoughtful, but smiles at him as he takes her hand in his. They come into fore., CAMERA PANNING ALONG TO FOLLOW as they make a turn at foot of garden and walk along shore of lake talking.

> FRANKENSTEIN
> It's like heaven to be with you again -
>
> ELIZABETH
> (wistfully)
> Heaven wasn't so far away all along -
>
> FRANKENSTEIN
> (a little brooding)
> I know, I know - but my work - those horrible days and nights - I couldn't think of anything
>
> ELIZABETH
> (interrupting him with a gentle smile)
> You're not going to think of those any more - You promised.
>
> FRANKENSTEIN
> (resolutely)
> Of course - we're going to think of nothing but ourselves - our wedding day -

He slips his arm around her waist, drawing her a little closer to him as they walk on.

> DISSOLVE THROUGH TO

H-2 EXT. LAKE SUNSET
     MED WIDE ANGLE
     Shooting on angle from shore
     to include part of the wide
     sweep of the lake and
     a canoe containing Elizabeth
     and Frankenstein. Great old
     willows line the curing bank,
     their drooping branches over-
     hanging the water, brushing
     it with soft tendrils. The canoe
     is drifting aimlessly along the
     shore under the trees. Elizabeth   (SOUND OF BELLS)
     is leaning back in Frankenstein's
     arms, her eyes closed. A look of
     great peace and happiness is on
     his face. From somewhere in the
     hazy distance comes the sound of
     church-bells.

                    ELIZABETH

                Listen - the Angelus -

                    FRANKENSTEIN
                        (with a sigh)

                The long day is over.

He bends down and touches
her hair with his lips - the
canoe continues to drift along
beneath the overhanging
willows - one by one the low
branches drop into place behind the stern of the canoe,
slowly blotting it from sight.

                            FADE OUT.

SEQUENCE "I"

FADE IN TO:

I-1 INT. LABORATORY AT MILL. NIGHT
LARGE CU MEDICAL CHART ON WALL

The chart, quite large and drawn
in pen-and-ink, shows several views
of the Monster's brain and heart -
cross-sections, etc. - all labelled
with notes i Waldman's precise
handwriting. A pencil is checking
a line of one of the convolutions
as CAMERA MOVES BACK TO MED..
CLOSE SHOT, picking up Waldman
as he lowers the pencil from the chart
and checks back to large ledger he
is making notes in. Frankenstein's
work-table has been cleared of all
the scientific apparatus and is
now littered with a conglomerate
assortment of note-books, sheaves
of papers, a big journal pen-and-ink
anatomical sketches, etc.
Waldman, perched up in front of the
table on the high stool which was
formerly Fritz's, looks haggard and
worn, as if he has been working for
long hours at his self appointed
task. The light of a small adjustable
lamp throws his face into grotesque
shadows. He lays his pencil aside
presses his finger tips tiredly
against his temples, and looks around
over his shoulder with a heavy sigh
of fatigue.

DISSOLVE THROUGH TO

I-2 INT. LABORATORY. WIDE ANGLE

matching action as Waldman turns
around and looks across at the
operating table, which occupies
its usual place in the center of
the room. The body of the Monster
is lying on the operating table
half-covered with a rubber sheet
head, shoulders, and arms exposed.
The room is dark except for the
adjustable lamp over the
work-table and a small, shaded
drop-light above the operating
table. Waldman gets down from his
stool and Xes to the operating
table, CAMERA PANNING TO FOLLOW
INTO CLOSE SHOT. Here he lifts
one of the Monster's arms and
checks his pulse

I-2   (CONTINUED)

- then he raises Monster's eyelid gently with his thumb. The monster appears to be in a state of complete unconsciousness. Waldman studies him thoughtfully for a moment then utters a grunt of satisfaction and Xes back to work table. CAMERA PANNING BACK. He flips back the pages of a large journal and starts to make a careful entry in ink.

I-3   CU INSERT JOURNAL

spread open, double-width left-hand page filled with Waldman's fine precise handwriting. Pen is writing carefully:

     Tuesday (cont.)
 2:30 A.M.
 Subject still in state of anesthesia as per injection of 5:00 - 9:20-12:30

 Note increased resistance necessitating stronger and more frequent injections

 However, will perform cranial dissection at once -

I-4   INT. CLOSE SHOT AT TABLE

matching action of 1-2 as Waldman completes his entry and turns toward small surgical carrier containing his instruments and starts to take them out of their cases

I-5   INT. CLOSE SHOT MONSTER'S FACE

His eyes start to flicker slowly open - he stares blankly at the ceiling with no trace of intelligence in them.

I-6   INT. WIDE ANGLE

    Waldman has completed the task of laying out his surgical instruments, and now wheels the carrier over to operating table, moving with swift, silent efficiency. CAMERA PANS WITH HIM INTO MED. CLOSE SHOT AT OPERATING TABLE. He stands with his back half-turned to the operating table - takes each bit of shinning steel and starts to sterilize them.

I-7   INT. FLASH CU MONSTER'S FACE

    as he gradually returns to full consciousness. Out of scene we hear the clink of the instruments as Waldman dips them into his sterilizing apparatus. Monster turns his eyes slowly in Waldman's direction, but does not move otherwise.

(CLINK OF INSTRUMENTS AGAINST GLASS)

I-8   INT. FLASH CLOSE SHOT TABLE,

    half screened by waldman's body - as seen from Monster's point of view a glimpse of the steel knives and scalpels. Waldman lays a particularly vicious looking knife down, after testing blade.

I-9   INT FLASH CU MONSTER'S FACE

    as an expression of fear flashes across it. His eyes roll from side to side as if seeking a way of escape. Suddenly aware of a movement on Waldman's part, Monster closes eyes quickly, simulating unconsciousness.

I-10   INT. MED. CLOSE SHOT OPERATING TABLE

matching action as Waldman
turns and glances at the
Monster, almost as if suspect-
ing that something is wrong -
then, continuing to contemplate
the recumbent figure, he starts
to pull on his surgical gloves.
The Monster remains very still
eyes closed. Waldman turns back
to carrier and again bends over
it, back half-turned to operating table. The Monster, with
quick agility, rises on one
elbow - his free arm shoots out
and hooks suddenly around Waldman's neck, squeezing it with a
sharp, vice-like grip. Waldman
utters a short, strangled
grunt and thrashes out wildly with his arms, twisting
and squirming. The Monster,
without relaxing his hold,
rises to a sitting position
and reaches out with his other
hand to seize Waldman's throat.

I-11   INT. LARGE CU MONSTER

an expression of savage triumph
on his face as he throttles
Waldman. Waldman's inarticulate
gurgling

I-12   INT. FLASH LARGE CU
        WALDMAN'S HEAD

upside down, the Monster's
gnarled fingers squeezing
his throat

FADE OUT.

SEQUENCE J

FADE IN TO:

H-1 INTERIOR PEASANT COTTAGE. .NIGHT

A typical mountain cottage, rustic and simple, with homely, handmade furniture. There is a good-sized fireplace at one end of the room, in which a fire crackles cheerfully. Adjoining the fireplace is a low rustic double bed. At one side of the room is a door leading into a small bedroom beyond. This door is closed. Johann, a peasant of about 30, is drinking beer as he sprawls in a comfortable chair beside a wooden table above which hangs an oil lamp, suspended by chains from the ceiling. His wife, Gretel, moves blithely about the room, completing the day's work preparatory to going to bed. She is a strong, buxom girl of about 24 and wears the peasant garb, with a black-laced bodice and fresh white blouse.

At FADE IN, the first thing we see is a LARGE CU BOWL OF BEER, supported by the thick hands of Johann, as he tilts it upward, draining it with gurgling satisfaction. CAMERA MOVES SLOWLY BACK, picking up Johann in CU, lowering the bowl, which he places on the table beside him, and wipes the foaming lips with the back of his hand. Then, with a sigh of deep satisfaction, he takes up his long-stemmed pipe from the table - puffs at it - finds it has gone out and starts to re-light it.

CAMERA, WHICH HAS BEEN MOVING SLOWLY BACK, now picks up Gretel, as she passes across fore., humming to herself. She and Johann exchange significant smiles - she indicates bedroom door (off-scene) and Xes toward it, Johann turning to watch her with a genial, expectant air.

CAMERA PANS WITH GRETEL TO CLOSE SHOT BEDROOM DOOR - she pauses at door and then opens it part of the way, slowly, cautiously - peer into the dim room beyond - CAMERA, STILL IN MOTION CONTINUES ON PAST HER INTO CLOSE SHOT TWO CHILDREN asleep on a trundle bed.

(CONTINUED)

J-1   (CONTINUED)

    They are two and three yeas old, respectively - curly-haired, adorable-looking youngsters - lying back to back. The light from the partly-opened door cuts obliquely across their bed, but not on their faces.
CAMERA MOVES QUICKLY BACK TO GRETEL, as she closes the door and looks back over her shoulder towards Johann with an intimate smile - nods and starts to unlace her bodice.

J-2   INTERIOR WIDE ANGLE,

    matching action as Johann, in fore., rises slowly from his chair - stretches - and then, with a broad grin upon his face, moves to fireplace and quietly knocks out his pipe. Gretel, in b. g., Xes to mirror hanging on a wall above the wooden chest of drawers, and starts to undress for the night, removing bodice and blouse. Johann places his pipe on the mantel and, turning to bed, draws down the covers - then looks across at Gretel.

J-3   EXT. L. S. CLEARING. NIGHT

    A clearing in the woods, about a couple of acres, where Johann has felled the trees and cultivated his small domain. On far side of clearing is the little cottage, a wisp of smoke curling lazily from the chimney, a light gleaming invitingly through the window. At one side of the cottage is a small truck-garden - behind, a low shed for the livestock. The low bushes in immediate fore. are parted abruptly and the head and shoulders of the Monster appear. She crouches, back to camera, in menacing silhouette, as if he has suddenly come upon this little dwelling and has paused to reconnoiter. His head moves from side to side, thoughtfully. Then he starts forward, rising to his full height, moving swiftly towards the cottage.

J-4   INT. COTTAGE.
      CLOSE SHOT GRETEL AT MIRROR

      She stands in her chemise and skirt,
      running a comb though her hair,
      which she has unbound and which
      hangs in flaxen luxuriance almost
      to her waist. Although pretending
      to be oblivious to Johann's presence,
      she is keeping an eye on him in the mirror.

J-5   INT. COTTAGE. CLOSE SHOT JOHANN

      as he removes his corduroy vest,
      and throws it carelessly over a chair,
      watching Gretel admiringly all the
      while, with a look of frank
      anticipation. Then he starts to open
      his shirt at the throat, Xing out
      of scene towards his wife.

J-6   INT. MED. CLOSE SHOT

      Gretel at mirror, combing her hair
      and humming to herself - Johann
      comes slowly into scene - stands watch-
      ing her for a moment with an indulgent
      air, and then leans down and kisses
      her, with a resounding smack, upon her
      bare shoulder. She laughs and pushes
      him playfully away. Undaunted, he
      grabs her and swings her around into
      his strong arms. There is a brief
      good-natured tussle - she glances over
      her shoulder towards the door of the
      bedroom where the children are sleeping
      with air of rebuke and protest:

                    GRETEL

                    Sh-h-h! Johann - !

      He releases her - she turns back to
      mirror and starts combing her hair
      again. He stands behind her.
      impatient, hardly able to keep his
      eager hands off her - then teasingly
      lifts one shoulder-strap of her
      chemise and drops it off her shoulder -
      she slaps his hand, but allows the
      strap to remain hanging.

J-7   INT. CU WINDOW

The dark outline of the Monster's head and shoulders appear just above the level of a row of flower pots on the sill outside. CAMERA MOVES SWIFTKY FORWARD TO LARGE CU MONSTER'S EYES, watching as the light from the lamp on the table is reflected in them - the rest of his face dim in the shadow.

J-8   INT. COTTAGE
       CLOSE SHOT JOHANN AND GRETEL

He reaches around and slips off the other shoulder strap - the chamise slips from her shoulders - she makes an involuntary movement with her arms to keep it from falling to the floor, laughing:

            GRETEL

        Johann - Johann - !

Becoming dominant now, he takes her by the shoulders - takes the comb away from her and throws it aside - then starts to push her gently, but emphatically towards the bed in the corner - when she continues to resist he imitates her previous warning gesture - puts a finger to his lips, indicating the closed bedroom door - then continues to push her out of scene.

J-9   INT. FLASH LARGE CU WINDOW

as eyes of the Monster widen.

J-10   INT. COTTAGE
       CLOSE SHOT END OF BED

The middle portion of Johann's body half-shielding Gretel from camera, moves across scene up towards head of the bed. CAMERA REMAINS IN CU OF END OF BED - there is the sound of the bed-spring squeaking - the mattress sags in towards the middle as the two bodies (out of camera) sink down upon it - we hear a smothered exclamation or two - a short, triumphant laugh from Johann - then the chemise is flung into camera, draping itself rakishly over foot of bed.

J-11   INT. FLASH VERY LARGE CU EYES

      as Monster watches from outside.

J-12   INT. LARGE CU ON BED

      Just the two faces of Johann and Gretel, very large and filling the screen, one above the other - Johann laughing in a low, excited tone - Gretel smiling up at him, acquiescent, waiting. Suddenly, from out of scene, there is a crash - a shattering of glass - a splintering and rending of the framework of the window. An expression of startled terror flashes into the two smiling faces.

J-13   INT. FLASH LARGE CU JOHANN

      rising into camera from bed.

J-14   INT. FLASH LARGE CU GRETEL

      slightly hidden behind Johann's body which almost fills screen arms clasped over her bosom, her eyes wide with terror.

J-15   INT. FLASH CLOSE SHOT MONSTER

      who has just clambered in through the wrecked window and is advancing into camera, eyes gleaming beastially, long arms outstretched to grapple. Johann's cry and Gretel's scream over scene.   (JOHANN'S CRY - GRETEL'S SCREAM

J-16   INT WIDE ANGLE ROOM

      Camera shooting from floor (25mm. lens) - Johann and Gretel in defensive attitudes at bed in b.g. as Monster, looming large in fore., advances towards them, moving warily. Johann moves quickly to one side, as if to draw him into combat away from Gretel - Gretel sinks back upon bed, cowering there. The Monster moves in quickly upon Johann, blotting him out of camera behind his huge body - there is a confused movement in b. g. as   (CONTINUED)

J-16 (CONTINUED)

    Monster gets grip on Johann - then raises him in his mighty arms and hurls him into corner out of camera.

J-17 INT. FLASH CU CORNER

    as Johann's body hurtles into scene and crashes into corner, a crumpled, lifeless heap. Gretel's scream over scene.   (GRETEL'S SCREAM)

J-18 INT. FLASH HUGE CU MONSTER

    turning and going for Gretel moves into camera with savage menace.

J-19 INT FLASH CLOSE SHOT BED

    Gretel tries to slither out of the way, screaming in stark terror. (GRETEL'S SCREAMS)

J-20 INT. MED SHOT

    matching action as Monster advances and snatches out - she leaps aside to avoid him - he follows her relentlessly - grabs her and gets her - as he does so, they crash against the table, which goes over, lamp and all. The lamp smashes, plunging the room into total darkness. There is another scream from Gretel - then silence and darkness. There is another scream from Gretel - then silence and darkness - and then presently a faint moan and then silence again.

J-21 INT. BEDROOM. FLASH CLOSE SHOT CHILDREN

    sitting bolt upright in bed, arms around each other, trembling with fright, wide-eyed, listening, too terrified to utter a sound.

                          FADE OUT

SEQUENCE "K"

FADE IN TO:

K-1   EXT. MOUNTAIN TOP. DAY

A very beautiful shot, with the
figure of a peasant, in costume
standing against the sky, blowing
his Swiss horn.
> (NOTE: This type of horn, made
> and used by the Swiss peasants
> for the purposes of calling
> from mountain to mountain,
> either for calling to their
> herds or for communicating
> in other ways, is about eight
> feet long, curving gracefully
> from the mouthpiece to bell, which   (HORN SOUNDS
> rests on the ground. It pro-   THROUGH SCENE)
> duces a very harmonious and
> powerful tone)

At his feet lies his companion
also in peasant costume, a long
blade of grass between his teeth.
The floor of the valley stretches
out below, whilst on all
sides are the high peaks and
mountain ranges.

        DISSOLVE THROUGH TO

K-2   EXT. MOUNTAIN ROAD

descending into valley. A number
of peasants, men and women, all
in gala attire, are walking along,   (HORN)
laughing and talking.

        DISSOLVE THROUGH TO

EXT. MED. L.S. MOUNTAIN COTTAGE

shooting from road towards the
cottage. In the narrow dirt
road stands a bullock cart, with
its huge wooden wheels
and a team of bullocks hitched to   (HORN)
the wagon-tongue. Another group
of peasants are preparing to
depart - running in and out of
the cottage - calling gaily to
one another - children are clambering
into the cart - a scene of excitement
and preparation. The peasants call
to another group passing by in the
road.

138

K-3 (CONTINUED)

    CAMERA PANS AROUND TO ANGLE
    ON ROAD, shooting down, where we
    see additional groups of peasants
    all in holiday dress.

        DISSOLVE THROUGH TO

K-4 EXT. VILLAGE STREET DAY.
    CRANE SHOT

    The camera is moving slowly along the
    main street of the village, picking
    up various groups of merrymakers.
    The street is crowded - flags are
    flying - houses draped with garlands   (STREET NOISES -
    of flowers - sounds of laughter -   CHURCH BELLS, ETC)
    the music of a carousel - the sharp
    crack of rifles in an improvised
    shooting gallery -
    concessionaires crying the attractions
    everybody in a happy mood. Over the
    noises of the street there is the
    sound of church bells.
    CAMERA DROPS DOWN FROM ELEVATION
    AND PANS ACROSS TO A CENTRAL
    EUROPEAN GUIGNOL- MARIONETTE SHOW

    moving over the heads of a group of
    delighted children and their elders,
    who are watching with almost as
    much delight - CAMERA MOVES INTO
    CU BOOTH, as puppet flits about with
    his club, calling in his high
    falsetto voice:

        PUPPET
            Poor Judy's dead -
            poor Judy's dead!

    The Devil pops up into sight -
    there is an excited murmur from
    the small audience - puppet turns
    and sees the Devil - CAMERA STARTS
    MOVING AWAY as we hear Puppet speak

        PUPPET

            Who are you?

        DEVIL
            (in a sepulchral voice)
            I am the Devil.

    CAMERA PANS AWAY OVER THE HEADS
    OF THE CHILDREN as Puppet starts
    to belabor the Devil with his club
    squealing:

K-4   CONTINUED

             PUPPET

                              O-o-o-h - the Devil! The
                              Devil! Go back where you
                              belong! Take that - and
                              that!

CAMERA ZIGZAGS to other
side of the street, into
MED. CLOSE SHOT MAN WITH
DANCING BEAR. The dancing
bear is performing, to the
accompaniment of a tambourine,
before a large group of inter-
ested spectators.

CAMERA, NEVER PAUSING ALWAYS
ADVANCING SWINGS BACK ACROSS
THE STREET, to concession booth
where a fat, good-natured woman
with a pronounced mustache is
selling candy - children clustered
around - a big, sheepish-looking
mountaineer buys some candy and
offers it to his giggling feminine
companion - CAMERA SWINGS TO
THE OTHER SIDE OF STREET, to
a carousel, whirling children and
fat burghers alike - much yelling
and calling to their friends in
the crowd as they spin around on
their painted wooden animals and
gaudy golden chariots to the
wheezy rendition of a Vienese
Waltz - CAMERA PANS UP THE SIDE
OF THE STREET, now to an open-air
shooting gallery, hastily thrown
up, constructed of canvas, where
several young bloods are trying
their skill - CAMERA CONTINUES
PANNING on past the village - add-
itional tables have been set out
to accommodate the crowd - the big
barrel of beer outside is receiving
plenty of attention as the inn-
keeper and his assistants rush
around with foaming steins and
tankards.

CAMERA SWINGS AROUND AND ACROSS
STREET TOWARDS BARON FRANKEN-
STEIN'S HOUSE. This house is set
a little apart from the other
dwellings, looming up quite impressively at the end of the street,
possibly the last house, commanding
the village thoroughfare.

I-4   (CONTINUED)

    The house stands almost flush with the street, but to the far side and behind we catch a glimpse of the park and gardens running down to the lake, as seen in previous sequence. The Baron and Victor are standing on a balcony above, watching the gay scene below. CAMERA ZOOMS UP TO CLOSE SHOT ON BALCONY Both men are dressed for the wedding. The Baron is beaming and in high fettle - Victor is grave and subdued. It is anything but a festive occasion for him, but hi is doing his best to conceal this true feelings.

> baron
> (indicating the villagers)
>
> This is a great day for them all, down there! They've watched Henry and Elizabeth grow up together -

Victor nods - CAMERA STARTS TO
MOVE PAST THEM TOWARDS INTERIOR

            DISSOLVE THROUGH TO

K-5   INT. LIVING ROOM CHALET

    as CAMERA CONTINUES MOVING FORWARD across the room, showing the elaborate decorations for the wedding reception - great banks of flowers everywhere, etc. - CAMERA MOVES TO CLOSE SHOT CLOSED DOOR, which as camera approaches, opens, and a maid-servant hurries out, excited and flustered by the importance of the occasion. CAMERA CONTINUES ON THROUGH DOOR. Elizabeth stands before a long mirror, in her wedding gown - two other maids are on their knees, arranging the bridal veil, which sweeps to the floor in graceful, flowing lines. CAMERA CONTINUES INTO CLOSE SHOT ELIZABETH'S FACE staring into the mirror. Her eyes are sad but resigned. She rouses from her apathy, CAMERA MOVING BACK TO MED. SHOT - says to one of the maids:

> ELIZABETH
>
> Open a window - it's stifling in here -

Maid rises obediently and Xes
to window.

K-6   EXT. CLOSE SHOT AT WINDOW

As maid opens it - we see the room beyond, with Elizabeth and the other maid. As first maid turns away from the window, CAMERA PANS QUICKLY ALONG SIDE OF HOUSE TO CLOSE SHOT ANOTHER WINDOW, open with Frankenstein standing framed in it, looking off towards the mountains. He, also, is dressed for the ceremony. DOUBLE EXPOSE OVER SCENE a long shot of the watch-tower, silhouetted against the sky - then another DOUBLE EXPOSE OF A LARGE CU WALDMAN'S face, which melts into an even larger CU of the Monster. Frankenstein turns - FADE OUT DOUBLE EXPOSE QUICKLY - he draws the windows shut with a sharp gesture, as if to banish his thoughts

(SOUND OF HORN VERY FAINT IN THE DISTANCE)

DISSOLVE THROUGH TO

K-7   EXT. FLASH MOUNTAIN TOP

Peasant blowing his horn - DOUBLE EXPOSE mountain road, with peasants going along towards the village - TRIPLE EXPOSE still another group with bullock carts and other conveyances - then

(SOUND OF HORN OVER TRIPLE EXPOSE TRIPLE EXPOSE OR OR QUICK DISSOLVES)

DISSOLVE THROUGH TO

K-8   EXT. L.S. CABIN NEAR MOUNTAIN LAKE

a small picturesque cabin belonging to Ludwig, the Bear-Hunter - there is an atmosphere of peaceful remoteness, of serenity, about it. On one side. heavy woods descend to the shores of the lake. Ludwig and his little five-year old daughter, Maria, are in front of the cabin - both in holiday garb. He picks her up in his arms.

DISSOLVE THROUGH TO

K-9   EXIT. SHOT CABIN

matching action as Ludwig swings the little girl up in the air and down again - she shrieks delightedly - a happy, intimate little scene. He lowers her to a bench outside of the cabin door and says, admonishly:

K-9   (CONTINUED)

    Ludwig picks up rifle or shot gun
    and says:

> LUDWIG
>> Now you are going to wait
>> here while I take a final
>> look at my bear-traps -
>> and then we will go to the
>> village -
>
> MARIA
>> (anxiously)
>
> You won't be long?
>
> LUDWIG
>> (laughingly)
>
> No, no -
>> (preparing to go)
>
> - and if Hans or Emil should
> come by, say to them that I
> am returning soon.

    he kisses her and starts off -
    she slides down from the bench
    and stands watching him, with a
    little pout.

K-10   WIDE ANGLE

    as Ludwig strikes out towards the
    edge of the woods - turns and looks
    back, waving to Maria and smiling.

K-11   EXT. CLOSE SHOT MARIA,

    her pout giving way to a smile,
    as she waves back calling:

> MARIA
>
> Don't be long!

K-12   EXT. L.S.

    as seen from Maria's angle -
    Ludwig shouts back something
    encouraging and strikes off
    into the woods, carrying rifle.

K-13   EXT. MED. CLOSE SHOT MARIA

as she sits down with a woebegone, but very resolute, air on the doorstep of the cabin to await Ludwig's return. Her eyes are watching the road that passes by the side of the cabin, quite a little distance away - suddenly her attention is drawn to -

K-14   EXT. L.S. ROAD,

as seen from cabin. A crowd of peasants go by, some on foot - a bullock-cart laden with children - they call and wave gaily to Maria, their voices indistinguishable in the distance.

K-15   EXT. CABIN REVERSE ANGLE

lake in b.g. Maria gets up and runs a few steps after the departing group - then stops and stands undecided, looking around for something to amuse her while she is waiting - starts aimlessly towards the shore of the lake.

K-16   EXT. WOODS FLASH MED. SHOT

Ludwig hurrying through woods - comes into fore., where there is a bear-trap - pauses to lean down and examine it.

K-17   EXT. MED. SHOT SHORE OF LAKE.

In the shallows by the shore are a number of water-lilies - also tall iris growing by the water's edge. Maria into scene - starts plucking the iris.

K-18   EXT. SHORE OF LAKE,

        a little further along - a spot where the underbrush and tall grass comes down to the edge of the water. The grass and bushes part, and we see the monster. He is hot and disheveled. He gets down on his hands and knees and starts to drink from the lake, like an animal. Then he lifts up his head, his jaws dripping, and glances off along shore- sees -

K-19   EXT. SHORE OF LAKE. MED. L.S.

        as seen from Monster's point of view. Through tall grass we catch a glimpse of Maria, gathering her flowers.

K-20   EXT SHORE OF LAKE.

        Monster watches for a moment - then rises to his feet, and starts slowly towards maria, sloshing along through the water. CAMERA PANS AROUND AND FOLLOWS HIM SLOWLY, Maria in b.g., Monster approaching, parting the reeds and cat-tails as he goes.

K-21   EXT. MED. SHOT SHORE OF LAKE

        Maria in fore., picking flowers - Monster comes into scene and stands watching her from the lake - she becomes aware of his presence and glances up.

K-22   EXT. FLASH CU MARIA

        as she sees Monster - at first she is startled - then, as her eyes take in his huge, ungainly, dripping figure, she looks surprised and perplexed.

                          MARIA
                    Who are you?

K-23   EXT. FLASH CU MONSTER,

    looking at her without moving
    a strange, bemused expression
    in his eyes.

K-24   EXT CU MARIA

    smiling timidly at him - says:

                  MARIA
                      I am Maria

K-25   EXT FLASH CU MONSTER

    still staring at her with the
    same odd expression on his face.

K-26   EXT. MED. CLOSE SHOT

    Maria looks up at the Monster, a
    little puzzled by his silence.
    He hasn't moved, but still stands
    regarding her as if he'd never seen
    anything quite like her before.
    She holds up an iris and says:

                  MARIA

                  Would you like on of my
                  flowers?

K-27   EXT. CU MONSTER,

    his eyes dropping from Maria's
    face to the flower she is holding
    up for him. Without changing the
    expression of his face, he starts
    to advance towards her.

K-28   EXT. CU MARIA

    holding up the flower smiling.
    The Monster's shadow falls
    across her face - then his two
    hands come into CU, reaching
    towards her.

                  FADE OUT

SEQUENCE "L"

L-1 INT. LIVING ROOM CHALET. DAY
LARGE CU MANTEL ABOVE FIREPLACE.

On a background of faded blue velvet, under a glass bell, is a wreath of imitation orange blossoms, and on each side of the wreath, a small boutonniere of the same. Beside the glass case is a small ivory painting of the Baron as a young man, and his bride, Frankenstein's mother. Baron's hand comes into CU, just lifting the glass bell off as we DISSOLVE IN - his voice over scene as CAMERA MOVES BACK TO MED. SHOT, disclosing the Baron, with a twinkle in his eye, turning from the mantel to Frankenstein, who is standing nearby with Victor. On an adjoining table is a dusty old bottle of kirschwasser, and three glasses, filled.

          BARON
    -for four generations, Victor, these orange blossoms have been worn at the wedding the boutonniere for the groom, the wreath for the bride -

Places the boutonniere in his son's buttonhole - then steps back, beaming.

    So!

Turns back to mantel and takes down the wreath, handling it with tender reverence, musing.

    Thirty years ago - I placed this on your mother's head -

The two young men stand in silence, eyes averted, respecting his memories - then the Baron rouses and, smiling, hands it to Frankenstein saying:

    And now you will do the same for one who is - almost as fair -

Frankenstein takes the wreath quietly - Baron moves across to where the glasses are standing on the table - CAMERA SWINGS AROUND TO WIDER ANGLE, GROUP STILL IN FORE., but shooting now towards the large double doors leading to the entrance hall. The Baron hands a glass to Victor

L-1   (CONTINUED)

                    BARON

                        And now - a toast -

Hands glass to Frankenstein and
then, taking the third for himself
raises it aloft with a smile saying:

                    BARON

                        My dear boy - to your lovely
                        bride - and to a son for the
                        House of Frankenstein -

As they all raise their glasses
the double doors in b.g. fly open
with a crash and a man stands
there. They wheel, startled

L-2   INT. CLOSE HOST IN DOORWAY

The man is the spectacled secretary
seen in the University sequence,
talking to Victor and Waldman.
He is in a state of wild excitement,
his clothing disheveled - flashes
a swift glance around at the three
men and cries, almost accusingly:

                    SECRETARY

                        Which of you is Henry
                        Frankenstein?

L-3   INT FLASH MED. SHOT GROUP,

as Frankenstein says:

                    FRANKENSTEIN

                        I am.

L-4   INT. LARGE CU SECRETARY
        as he gasps out:

                    SECRETARY

                        Doctor Waldman has been
                        butchered!

and sinks into a chair near
the door in a state of collapse.

L-5   EXT. ROAD LEADING TO VILLAGE.
      MED CLOSE SHOT LUDWIG,

      walking slowly, tragically, towards
      camera. In his outstretched arms
      he holds the limp, dripping form
      of little Maria.
      CAMERA MOVES BACK, keeping pace
      with tempo of his progression, as he
      advances.

                DISSOLVE THROUGH TO

l-6   ext. med. l. s. end of village street
       MOVING SHOT

      as Ludwig comes walking with his
      slow, tragic tread up to the out-
      skirts of crowd of peasants in fore.
      Marionette show drawing laughs from
      the crowd, mostly children. One of
      the peasants happens to turn and
      see Ludwig - calls attention of the
      others - they all draw back to make
      way for him to pass - a couple of wo-
      men try to hide the weight of the
      dead girl from the younger children.
      All talking and laughter ceases.

L-7   EXT. CLOSE SHOT MARIONETTE SHOW

      The puppets drop - the head of the
      proprietor appears over the top of
      the booth, watching with his pendu-
      lous jaw agape.

L-8   EXT. MOVING CLOSE SHOT LUDWIG

      advancing - on both sides of him
      we see the peasants turn - stare -
      and draw back in horror. Ludwig
      passes by the dancing bear show,
      CAMERA NEVER PAUSING.

L-9   EXT. MED. SHOT GROUP AROUND BEAR

      They all turn, the bear forgotten, all
      eyes on Ludwig - the trainer pauses
      in the very act of tossing a ball for
      the bear to catch and looks stupidly
      at Ludwig - bear drops heavily down
      upon its four feet.

L-10   EXT. MOVING SHOT OF LUDWIG,

        walking with same measured tread towards camera, which precedes him - his eyes filled with tears, face grim, looking neither to the right nor to the left. All around, silence closes in behind him as he passes. - behind him, passing out of focus, we see the shocked villagers.

L-11   EXT. FLASH CLOSE SHOT LITTLE GIRL,

        hiding behind her mother's skirts

L-12   EXT. MOVING SHOT LUDWIG

        as he passes by the candy concession

L-13   EXT. FLASH CLOSE SHOT CANDY CONCESSION,

        as the fat woman drops candy she has been selling and points a far forefinger. Everybody at the counter turns and stares.

L-14   EXT. FLASH MOVING SHOT LUDWIG,   (SOUND OF HAND ORGAN, GROWING LOUDER WITH LUDWIG'S APPROACH)

        walking into camera. Sound of hand-organ comes into scene.

L-15   EXT. MED SHOT ORGAN-GRINDER

        He is play merry tune as three or four children dance. The music comes to an abrupt stop as organ-grinder see Ludwig - he crosses himself - children back away - one of them utters a little scream, but this too, is abruptly muffled as one of her older companions claps a hand over her mouth admonishingly.

L-16   EXT. MOVING SHOT LUDWIG,

        passing the village inn.

L-17   EXT. MED. SHOT FRONT OF VILLAGE INN

    as all activity ceases and everybody stares at the passing figure of Ludwig. Two or three half-rise from their places at the little tables - waiters with their fingers looped around four or five stein handles stop in their tracks - drinks on tables are abandoned - all heads are turned, following Ludwig as he goes by. An ominous silence settles down over everybody.

L-18   EXT. MOVING SHOT LUDWIG,

    He approaches the carousel-music from carousel comes into scene, growing louder.   (CAROUSEL MUSIC GROWING LOUDER)

L-19   EXT. MED. SHOT CAROUSEL

    The man at the control shuts off the power - music trails off into discordant silence - the carousel wheezes to a full stop everybody gaping.   (CAROUSEL MUSIC DIES AWAY IN DISCORDS)

L-19A EXT. CLOSE SHOT CAROUSEL

    a horse coming to full stop and CAMERA PANS UP to face of child rider.

L-20   EXT. FLASH LARGE CU FAT PEASANT

    eating a waffle - he pauses, waffle half-way to his mouth.

L-21   MOVING SHOT LUDWIG

    as he nears the shooting gallery. Staccato volley of shots heralds his approach.   (SHOTS FROM SHOOTING GALLERY)

L-22   EXT. MED. SHOT SHOOTING GALLERY,

    as the firing tapers off and everybody turns

L-23   EXT. VILLAGE STREET. MOVING SHOT

from slight elevation, just high enough to look down over the heads of the crowd. Ludwig advancing into camera, which now starts moving away from him at a slightly faster tempo - everybody in fore. turning to see what's going on - the peasants are falling in behind him - a great crowd gathering, from which an ominous murmur starts to arise, growing louder and louder.

L-24   INT. LIVING ROOM CHALET

Baron, Victor, and Frankenstein listening in attitudes of concernation as the secretary finishes giving his account of the discovery of Waldman's murder.

                    SECRETARY

                        - the laboratory was
                        wreaked - everything
                        smashed to bits - Wald-
                        man lying in the midst
                        of it all - torn to pieces!

He drops into a chair, exhausted. Baron turns to get him a drink. Victor looks at Frankenstein in deep horror.

                    VICTOR

                        The Monster!

                    FRANKENSTEIN
                            (brokenly)
                        Waldman - my dear old
                        friend -
                            (Turns away)

baron shoves a drink into the secretary's trembling hand.

                    BARON

                        Here -

                    FRANKENSTEIN
                            (in an agony of remorse)
                        All my doing.

                            (LOW ROAR OF CROWD
                            FROM OUTSIDE GROWING
                            LOUDER)

L-24 (CONTINUED)

                    VICTOR

               What's that? Listen!

They all listen, turning
towards the windows leading
out upon the balcony.

                         (ROAR GROWS LOUDER
                         AND MORE MENACING)

                    BARON

               There's something wrong -

They rush towards the balcony,
flinging open the windows -
CAMERA FOLLOWS SWIFTLY INTO
CLOSE SHOT - all backs are
turned to camera as they look
off down the street.

                    VICTOR
                       (pointing)
               Look - in front of the
               burgomeister's house!

L-25 EXT. L.S. FROM BALCONY

      as seen by group. A great crowd
      is in front of the burgomeister's
      house, roaring with rage at sight
      of Ludwig, as he stands just
      beneath the burgomeister's balcony
      a little apart from the rest,
      holding the body of the little Maria.

L-26 EXT. BALCONY BURGOMEISTER'S HOUSE

      The windows are hurriedly opened and
      the burgomeister steps out to face
      the crowd. He has been dressing,
      and had not had time to slip on his
      coat. He carries a hairbrush in his
      hand. He holds up his hand and
      shouts:

                    BURGOMEISTER

               Silence! Please! Silence!

                         (ROAR DIES SLOWLY AWAY)

Burgomeister looks bewildered -
then sees Ludwig standing below.

L-27   EXT. CLOSE SHOT LUDWIG

shooting down from balcony down. He
raises his arms, bringing the body
of the girl up a little into the
camera. Great tears are coursing   (ROAR FROM CROWD)
down his cheeks. At his gesture,
there is another roar from the crowd.

L-28   EXT. FLASH CU BURGOMEISTER

looking down at Ludwig, his face
filled with quick pity. For a
moment he does not speak - then
he says, with grave gentleness:

                    BURGOMEISTER

                My poor Ludwig -

Stops, unable to go on. Then a
look of bewilderment comes into
his eyes as he asks:

                Why do you bring her here
                to me?

L-29   EXT. CU LUDWIG

looking up at the burgomeister

                    LUDWIG

                She has been slain.

L-30   EXT. FLASH CU BURGOMEISTER

aghast.

L-31   EXT. FLASH CLOSE SHOT GROUP IN
        crowd

They are watching with grim faces
muttering and whispering among then-
selves.

L-32   EXT. FLASH CLOSE SHOT BALCONY

as Barn, Victor, and Frankenstein
watch and listen. Into Frankenstein's
face there is gradually creeping a
look of horrible certainty. Victor   (CROWD STARTS TO
and he exchange slow, significant   MUTTER AGAIN)
looks, then as Victor turns back to
watch the crowd, Frankenstein turns
Dazedly away, unwilling to have his
companions see the horror in his face.

L-33   EXT. L.S. STREET SHOOTING DOWN
       WIDE ANGLE

   as seen from balcony of Baron's
   house. The crowd surges forward
   towards the burgomeister, commencing their deep-throated roar again

L-34   EXT. FLASH ANOTHER GROUP IN CROWD

   A burly mountaineer cries out
   above the rumble of the crowd:

                MOUNTAINEER
             Find the murderer!

L-35   EXT. FLASH CU ANOTHER PEASANT

   crying excitedly:

                PEASANT

             A fiend is loose in the mountains!

                (ROAR INCREASES AT
                THIS)

L-36   EXT. FLASH CU BURGOMEISTER,

   trying to make himself heard
   above the cries of the raging
   mob:

                BURGOMEISTER

             Justice will be done!

L-37   EXT. L.S. CROWD

   Victor and Baron in silhouette, fore.
   as seen from balcony in fore., The
   peasants roar rising to a single full
   throated cry of fury.

                DISSOLVE THROUGH TO

SEQUENCE "M"

(ROAR OF CROWD
CARRIES OVER DISSOLVE
BECOMING LOUDER)

M-1   EXT. L.S. STREET NIGHT

This shot is an exact duplicate of
the preceding one, except that now
it is night. The lights in the
houses stream down over the heads
of the assembled mob in front of
the burgomeister's house. Every
window is filled with watchers.
The movement of the mob is more
restless, as if they were all   (SOLEMN TOLLING OF
anxious to be off on their hunt   CHURCH BELL ON A
for the killer. Torches are being   SINGLE NOTE.)
swiftly distributed. Above the
roar of the ground sounds the
occasional howling of hounds,
and with a grim note of sepulchral
insistence comes the steady tolling
of a church bell, at intervals of
about 15 seconds. CAMERA MOVES
BACK TO SHOW in immediate fore.,
Victor and the Baron stand on the   (TOLLING
balcony of the chalet, backs to
camera as before, silhouetted   OF
against the lurid radiance of the
torches.   BELL

                                    OVER

M-2   EXT. FLASH MOVING CLOSE SHOT GROUP   SCENES

with torches and flares - all the   UNTIL
men are carry weapons - rifles
clubs, scythes, etc. As CAMERA MOVES OTHERWISE
ACROSS GROUP,
                                    INDICATED)

            DISSOLVE THROUGH TO

M-3   EXT. FLASH CLOSE SHOT HOUNDS

A trio of them, huge beasts,
straining at their leashes.

M-4   EXT. FLASH MED. SHOT

Two village officials with a
large supply of pine torches
are passing them out to a
crowd of peasants who push
eagerly forward to get them.

M-5   EXT. CLOSE SHOT BURGOMEISTER

as he stands on his balcony, addressing the crowd. The light from the torches below flickers over his face as he exhorts the mob.

> BURGOMEISTER
>
> Search every ravine - every crevice - in the hills! The forest - the shores of the lake - the fiend must be found!

a roar of approval goes up from the crowd.

M-6   EXT. FLASH LARGE CU LUDWIG

listening with grim determination

M-7   EXT. CLOSE SHOT BURGOMEISTER

A servant appears at the burgomeister's elbow from within the house and whispers excitedly to him. Burgomeister turns again to the crowd - raises his hands for silence. The crowd quiets down momentarily as he announces:

> BURGOMEISTER
>
> Baron Frankenstein has posted a reward of ten thousand kronen - dead or alive.

Another roar goes up.

M-8   EXT. FLASH WIDE ANGLE ON STREET

as the crowd turns from beneath the burgomeister's house and starts moving up the street towards the hills - first slowly, sluggishly, due to the great press of people - then with increasing swiftness - torches bobbing the roar increasing.

M-10 EXT. FLASH CLOSE SHOT HOUNDS

as they leap forward, dragging their keeper with them.

M-11 INT. LIVING ROOM CHALET
MED. SHOT NEAR FIREPLACE

Frankenstein, in an attitude of utter despair and self-condemnation, is huddled in one corner of the divan before the fireplace his face in his hands. Elizabeth is doing her best to comfort him. She has removed her wedding gown and wears a simple frock.

    FRANKENSTEIN

    I'm the one who's guilty -

    ELIZABETH

    Henry, dear - you mustn't -

    FRANKENSTEIN

    There's blood on my hands - blood of peasants - little children -

Rises and takes her fiercely by the shoulders.

    Do you want to marry a murderer?

    ELIZABETH
    (distressed)

    Oh, don't - don't - !

She turns away, eyes filled with tears. Frankenstein moves agitatedly about - pauses

    (ROAR OF MOB OUTSIDE)

    FRANKENSTEIN
    (pointing grimly to window)

    Hear them, out there! They've gone mad!

Elizabeth listens, apprehensively. Frankenstein resumes his pacing - then stops and listens again - pressed his hands to his ears, exclaiming tensely:

    FRANKENSTEIN

    I created that Monster - I'll destroy him!

M-11 (CONTINUED)

          ELIZABETH
          (frantically trying to stop him)

      He'll destroy you - like all the others!

This speech brings them to door. Frankenstein flings open door leading to hall and looks down at her - just once - all the bitterness and agony in his heart bursting forth in one hysterical:

          FRANKENSTEIN

      Does it matter?

The exits, slamming the door behind him. Elizabeth pulls open the door and rushes out into the hall, screaming:

          ELIZABETH

      Henry! Come back! Come back!

M-12   INT. FLASH CLOSE SHOT ENTRANCE DOOR

slamming violently behind Frankenstein as he exits.

M-13   INT. HALL MED. SHOT

Living room door in b.g. Elizabeth runs a few steps down the hall into fore., crying again, desperately:

          ELIZABETH

      Henry!

At this, the Baron and Victor emerge hastily from the living room and hasten towards Elizabeth.

          VICTOR

      Elizabeth! What is it?

          ELIZABETH

      He's gone - he's gone! Stop him!

M-13   (CONTINUED)

   All three whirl around into
   camera, their faces filled
   with consternation.

M-14   EXT. CHALET. MED. SHOT. SIDE ANGLE

   Peasants surging past the
   front of the house, torches
   flaring. Frankenstein rushes
   out of the house and joins the
   group of marching men. As the
   peasants recognize him they
   welcome him with enthusiastic
   acclaim - crowd moves on, Frankenstein is in its midst.

M-15   EXT. STREET MOVING SHOT.

   Large body of peasants marching into camera, torches upraised. Among them is Frankenstein, a wild, desperate
   look in his eyes - as he marches
   into large CU

                DISSOLVE THROUGH TO

M-16   EXT. FLASH L.S. VILLAGE STREET

   shooting towards the hills.
   Broken groups of peasants
   with bobbing torches all moving
   up towards the hills.

                DISSOLVE THROUGH TO

M-17   EXT. HILLS. VERY L.S. REVERSE ANGLE

   looking down upon the village from
   elevation. The mob of peasants are
   spreading out, fan-wise, into three
   general groups - one group advancing
   straight towards the hills, the other
   two going to right and left.

                DISSOLVE THROUGH TO

M-18   HILLS MED. SHOT OVERHANGING ROCK

shooting up against the sky. Over the edge of this rock appears the head of the Monster.

                    DISSOLVE THROUGH TO

M-19   EXT. LARGE CU ROCK

profile shot, showing Monster looking down into the valley below, crouching there like some horrible gargoyle.

M-20   EXT FLASH VERY L.S. INTO VALLEY

showing the lines of peasants thinning out, almost in single file as they spread out around the base of the hills and start climbing up.

M-21   EXT. MED. SHOT VILLAGE CHURCH

A group of women and children are being herded into the church by a pair of husky-looking peasants with guns. Out of scene, the lines of men with their torches are still passing by, as evidenced by their moving shadows across the face of the building. The Baron and Victor comes into the scene with Elizabeth. who has thrown a light wrap over her frock. Both men look very worried and in a hurry to locate Frankenstein.

                    VICTOR

                        Don't stir out-of-doors
                        until we come for you -
                        You will be safe here my dear!

                    ELIZABETH

                        Don't worry about me! Find
                        Henry - hurry - before it's
                        too late.

The Baron pats her arm reassuringly - Victor presses her hand in silence unable to find words to express his feelings - they both exit, hurriedly falling in with a passing group of peasants Elizabeth watches them go, then slowly enters the church - the women falling back to allow her to pass.

M-22 INT VILLAGE CHURCH.

    A small, inexpensive set with plain whitewashed walls and crude, wooden appointments. The room is crowded with women and children, the children frightened and whimpering - the women in little knots of twos and threes, murmuring among themselves. The pews are filled — many are praying. In b.g. the village priest is offering up a prayer. The church is lit only by candles, which give a weird, unearthly effect to the scene. Elizabeth enters and stands with bowed head, praying silently. The village women watch her curiously with deep sympathy.

M-23 EXT. MED. SHOT STREET.

    Peasants going by - the Baron and Victor hail a group, who pause, holding torches aloft - they recognize him and fall back respectfully. The leader of the little group says, with grave deference:

                  LEADER

            A grim business, Herr Baron!

                BARON
                  (Nodding curtly)
            Is my son among you?

                SEVERAL VOICES

            No, Herr Baron... We haven't seen him... I think I saw him go that way, Herr Baron..

                BARON
                  (to Victor)
            Come - he must have gone on ahead -

    They exit, the peasants following.

M-24   EXT. HILLS.

A detachment of peasants with
torches, Frankenstein at their
head, have arrived at the edge
of the forest. Frankenstein
halts them with:

                    FRANKENSTEIN

                         Wait!

They obey, looking to him for
instructions.

                         half of you go around by the
                         lake - the rest of us will go
                         up this way -

There is a general murmur of
assent - the party separates
as he has ordered.

m-25   flash med. l. s. side angle

as Frankenstein and his men start
up the side of the hill through
the trees.

M-26   EXT. FLASH SHORE OF LAKE

About twenty men moving slowly
along the shore, their torches
reflected in the dark waters.

M-27   EXT. FLASH MED. CLOSE SHOT WOODS

The hounds pass before camera,
rushing through the underbrush,
the men holding their leashes
having difficulty in keeping
them back. The hounds start to
bay loudly.

M-28   EXT. CLOSE SHOT ROCK.

Monster leaning over the rock,
watching and listening. From
far below comes the sound of
the hounds, baying. The Monster
raises himself slowly to a
half-standing position, a look of fright   (SOUNDS OF DOGS IN
on his face as he hears the dogs   DISTANCE
coming nearer.

M-29   EXT. FLASH L.S. HILLS,

shooting down - very steep angle over jagged rocks and boulders. Group of peasants scrambling up over the rocks.

M-30   EXT ROCKS. MED. SHOT

as Monster, looking down, sees the peasants coming up - turns and flees further up the rocks.

M-31   EXT. FLASH L.S. WOODED SLOPES.

In and out among the trees, as far as the eye can penetrate the dark forest, we glimpse the torches flashing about - men calling back and forth to each other.

M-32   EXT. ROCKY HILLSIDE.

Another location, presumably at a point where the woods thin out and the rocky formation of the mountains begin. Frankenstein and his group climbing up past camera. Frankenstein has fallen back a little - finds it hard going, as if not as used to traversing these rocky places as the more nimble-footed peasants are.

M-33   EXT. MED SHOT LARGE ROCK

shooting on angle down the hill rock in immediate fore. Behind this rock crouches the Monster, watching the searching party come towards him. Certain now of his danger, his face wears a hunted animal cunning.

M-34   EXT FLASH MED. CLOSE SHOT
        HILLSIDE

Frankenstein in fore. - the others scrambling on up ahead of him. Large fissures and crevices are commencing to appear in the rocky surface of the hills. Frankenstein misses his footing and drops his torch.

FB

M-35   EXT. FLASH CLOSE SHOT DEEP CREVICE

as torch drops down into it and is extinguished.

M-36   EXT. CLOSE SHOT FRANKENSTEIN

With an exclamation of annoyance, he picks himself up and starts to try to retrieve his fallen torch. It is necessary for him to lie down flat and thrust his arm down into the crevice - in doing so, he gives his shoulder a sharp wrench - succeeds in getting the torch and then sits up and starts cursing his shoulder to see what has happened to the others.

M-37   EXT FLASH L.S. UP HILLSIDE
       REVERSE ANGLE

from Frankenstein's angle, as the last of the men are vanishing over the brow of the hill.

M-38   MED. SHOT NEAR LARGE ROCK.

Legs of the peasants passing in immediate fore. (25mm lens shot) - in b.g., lying flat on his belly, Monster is watching craftily. CAMERA MOVES FORWARD TO LARGE CU MONSTER'S FACE, as he follow progress of the men past his hiding place.

M-39   EXT. FLASH CLOSE SHOT FRANKENSTEIN

as he gets up and looks around - then seats himself on a convenient rock and attempts to re-light his torch.

M-40   EXT. FLASH VERY L.S. HILLS,

shooting down again towards the village. The last detachment of men leaving - village deserted behind them. Church bell is still tolling the single, insistent not as though all preceding scenes as indicated.

M-41   EXT. FLASH L.S. VILLAGE STREET

        The men are all gone now and the street is empty - lights burning in all the windows - doors left open - everything indicating the hurried departure.   (CHURCH BELL STILL TOLLING)

        DISSOLVE THROUGH TO

M-42   EXT. FLASH LARGE CU CHURCH BELL,

        tolling the one dismal note. This dies away as we

        DISSOLVE THROUGH TO

M-43   EXT. WIDE PANORAMIC SHOT HILLS

        A wide, striking vista of mountains and valley. All up and down the slopes of the hills are countless bobbing lights from the torches giving the effect of a gigantic man-hunt of hundreds of searching men.

        (NOTE: This effect need not necessarily entail the actual use of hundreds of men, as by using perhaps a hundred moving lights we can fill in for this brief shot with another hundred stationary ones etc.)

        DISSOLVE THROUGH TO

M-44   EXT. MOUNTAIN TOP

        shooting up. One of the peasant leaders is framed against the sky, while below him the others wait. He has his cupped hands to his mouth and is calling:

        LEADER

        Hallo -o-o-o-o-!

M-45   EXT. FLASH ANOTHER, LOWER, PEAK

        shooting down. The Baron and Victor, with their group, listen as the far echoes of the distant call sound eerily over the scene. Then the Baron cups his hands over his mouth and sends back an answering cry:

FB
M-45   (CONTINUED)

                    BARON

               Hallo-o-o-o-o!

M-46   EXT. ROCKY HILLSIDE.

        Monster slinking along - stops
        and listens as the echoes of
        the Baron's cry reach his ears -
        then slips away into the dark,
        keeping as close as possible
        to the shadows of the great rocks.

M-47   EXT. FLASH MED. SHOT FRANKENSTEIN.

        He has succeeded in lighting his
        torch again - gets up from the
        rock where he has been resting
        and favoring his wrenched shoulder,
        starts to trudge determinedly up
        the hill.

M-48   EXT. FLASH MED. SHOT HILLSIDE,

        Monster coming down into camera -
        as he reaches fore. he stops,
        peering ahead - then leaps out
        of sight behind a group of
        boulders.

M-49   EXT. FLASH HILLSIDE

        shooting down from Monster's
        point-of-view. Frankenstein
        coming up the hill.

M-50   EXT. FLASH LARGE CU MONSTER,

        recognizing Frankenstein, his
        sweaty face contorted with
        hate and malice. He draws
        himself up, ready to spring.

M-51   EXT MED. L.S. HILLSIDE

        shooting down. Monster behind
        rock in fore., back to camera,
        watching and waiting - up from
        b.g. Frankenstein approaching
        his torch held high.

M-52   EXT. MED SHOT AT ROCK. SIDE ANGLE,

    matching action as Frankenstein comes up the hill into scene. As he rounds the corner of the rock where the Monster is lurking, Monster leaps out into his path - Frankenstein starts back with a cry.

M-53   EXT. FLASH LARGE CU FRANKENSTEIN

    staring at Monster.

M-54   EXT. FLASH CU MONSTER

    coming slowly towards Frankenstein

M-55   EXT. MED. SHOT ANOTHER ANGLE,

    as Frankenstein retreats a step or two, thrusting his blazing torch at the Monster, who recoils with a snarl.

                  FRANKENSTEIN

                    Fire..! Fire..!

    Monster cowers - Frankenstein glances hastily around, still keeping torch levelled defensively - starts to call at the top of his voice.

                    FRANKENSTEIN

                    Hallo-o-o! ... Hallo-o-o!

M-56   EXT. WIDE ANGLE SMALL PLATEAU.

    At one side, the forest ends in a tangle of scrub oaks and heavy underbrush - in b.g. the rocky slopes extend up out of camera. The Baron and Victor and their men are coming down the side of the slope in b.g. just as another party breaks cover from the woods. The Baron peering through the darkness, hails the leader:

M-56 (CONTINUED)

                    BARON

                Emil - ?

                    EMIL
                  (calling)
              Ja, Herr Baron!

The two groups come together,
the light of their torches ming-
ling. CAMERA MOVES FORWARD INTO
MED. CLOSE SHOT BARON, VICTOR
and EMIL.

                    BARON
                  (anxiously)
          Have you seen my son?

Emil shakes his head stolidly.
The Baron looks disappointed
and worried.

M-57 EXT. MED. SHOT AT ROCKS.

Frankenstein still holding the
Monster at bay with his torch
and crying, more loudly, excitedly:

                FRANKENSTEIN

            Hallo-o-! . . . Hallo-o!

M-58 EXT. FLASH CLOSE SHOT MONSTER

    cowering against a rock, the
    flashing tip of the torch in scene,
    keeping him at his distance.

M-59 EXT. MED. SHOT PLATEAU.

Baron, Emil and Victor in fore.
- in b.g. the rest of the men
have dropped wearily to the
ground, snatching a brief rest
before pressing on.

                    BARON

          No signs of anything yet,
          Emil?

                    EMIL

          Nothing, Herr Baron, but -

M-59   (CONTINUED)

    Frankenstein's cry sounds faintly
    over scene, clipping Emil's speech   (FRANKENSTEIN'S CRY)
    short. Baron and Victor stiffen,
    listening.

                    BARON

              Listen!

Hold up his hand for silence.
In b.g. the low murmur of the
others ceases - everybody tense.

                    VICTOR

              That's Henry's voice!

Men in b.g. get to their feet
hurriedly, observing the renewed
tension.

                    BARON
                 (pointing)

              That way - !

                 (to the others)

              Come!

They all start to exit swiftly
in direction indicated by Baron.

M-60   EXT. FLASH LARGE CU FRANKENSTEIN

    calling again, at the top of
    his voice:

                    FRANKENSTEIN

              Hallo! Hallo! Hallo!

M-61   EXT. CLOSE SHOT MONSTER

    still shrinking away from the
    lighted end of the torch, which
    appears in scene. Suddenly, the
    flame starts to flicker out.
    Monster notices this and prepares
    to spring.

M-62   MED. SHOT

Frankenstein is looking around excitedly in all directions, trying to locate the lights of some of the searching parties. The torch continues to flicker out - Monster is creeping slowly, warily towards Frankenstein.

M-63   EXT. FLASH L.S. HILLS,

dark and deserted.

M-64   EXT. MED. SHOT ANOTHER ANGLE,

Monster is fore., edging towards Frankenstein. Frankenstein turns noes his furtive progress - then sees what is happening to his torch - frantically tries to revive the fire, but the torch is almost spent. He lunges at the Monster with the remains, shouting frantically:

              FRANKENSTEIN

           Back! Back! Down!

M-65   EXT. FLASH WOODS. SIDE ANGLE.

Baron, Victor, and the men rushing past camera towards Frankenstein.

M-66   EXT. MED. SHOT

Frankenstein with his back to camera - torch almost out - Monster advancing with an imbecilic, terrible smile of triumph. As Frankenstein backs into camera, CAMERA MOVES SLOWLY BACK.

M-67   EXT. FLASH CU STONE.

Frankenstein's foot, backing into scene, treads on stone, which becomes dislodged, rolling beneath foot and throwing Frankenstein off balance.

M-68   MED. SHOT,

    matching action as Frankenstein goes crashing to the ground. In one great leap, the Monster is upon him.

M-69   EXT. FLASH WOODS,

    shooting down from slight elevation. Baron, Victor, and men coming up rise of ground into camera.

M-70   EXT. ROCKY HILLSIDE

    Monster is clambering up the rocks, dragging the unconscious body of Frankenstein.

M-71   EXT. HILLSIDE NEAR ROCKS

    Same location as Scene M-32, where forest ends and the rocky slopes begin.
    Baron, Victor, and men emerge from the underbrush and halt for a moment - Baron and Victor call in opposite directions.

                  BARON

                Hallo-o-o-o!

                  VICTOR

                Hallo-o! Henry! Henry!

    They pause, waiting for an answer, but none comes.

M-72   EXT. ROCKY HILLSIDE. SIDE ANGLE.

    A location not far from the mountain top. Monster toils up past the camera, dragging Frankenstein's body with him.

M-73   EXT. HILLSIDE NEAR ROCKS.

    Baron, Victor,, and others looking around - then Baron turns to the men and says sharply:

M-73   (CONTINUED)

                    BARON

               Come along!

   and they all continue on up the
   side of the mountain.

M-74   EXT. CREST OF NEARBY HILL.

   Up over the hill from the other
   side burst a detachment of
   peasants with the torches -
   they line up along the ridge,
   scanning the surrounding
   territory. Suddenly leader
   points off, crying excitedly:

                    LEADER

               Look! Over there!

   The men crowd around, looking
   off in direction of his pointing
   finger.

M-75   EXT. FLASH VERY L.S. ROCKY HILLSIDE

   Against the whiteness of the
   rocks, the dark figures of the
   Monster and Frankenstein
   are seen, very small - The
   Monster crawling up over boulders
   and then pausing to turn back
   and drag Frankenstein's body up
   after him.

M-76   EXT. FLASH MED. SHOT CREST OF HILL

   as those in the rear of the party
   hasten forward - great excitement -
   leader shouts over his shoulder to
   them and they all dash away, scrambling swiftly down the side of the
   hill.

M-77   EXT. MED. SHOT NEAR TOP OF
       ROCKY HILLSIDE

   Monster has almost reached the top
   pauses for a moment to pull Frankenstein up after him - looks off -

M-78   EXT. FLASH L.S. TOWARDS
       ADJOINING HILL,

   as seen from Monster's point-of-view
   Men hurrying down side of hill
   into little ravine and up the
   other side towards camera.

M-79   EXT. FLASH MED. CLOSE SHOT MONSTER

   as he redoubles his efforts to reach
   the summit of the hillside.

M-80   EXT. ROCK LOCATION,

   recently vacated by Monster and
   Frankenstein. Baron, Victor, and
   the others come up the hill and
   pause momentarily near the big rock.

M-81   EXT. FLASH CLOSE SHOT HOUNDS,
   as they start to strain at their
   leashes, snarling and snapping
   - very excited.

M-82   EXT. CLOSE SHOT VICTOR AND BARON,

   as Victor indicates dogs - exclaims:

                       VICTOR

               Look - the hounds! They've
               picked up a trail!

M-83   EXT. ROCKS. WIDE ANGLE.

   Baron, Victor in fore. - Baron
   turns his attention to the hounds,
   who start to bay - Baron says to
   men holding them:

                       BARON

               Turn them loose!

   The men obey - hounds dash away
   up the rocky slope - a great cry
   goes up from the men as, headed
   by Victor and the Baron, they
   follow as fast as they can.
   CUT L.S. hounds dashing away
   up slope.

M-84   EXT. VERY L.S. CREST OF HILL,

shooting up at slight elevation from a spot as directly opposite as location permits. Framed against the skyline are the ruins of an old mill, which stands in the rocky clearing at the very top of the hill. The sails are torn in many places, hanging in shreds, yet whole enough to present sufficient resistance to the night breeze, before which they are lazily turning. The structure presents a gaunt, spectral appearance creating a grim effect of desolation and abandonment. Monster is seen just struggling up over the crest of the hill. From below come the baying of the hounds.
He appears to pause, listening - then flinging Frankenstein across his shoulder like a sack of meal, starts towards the mill on a run, crouching low.

(BAYING OF HOUNDS)

M-85   EXT. TOP OF MILL

shooting down towards ground. Monster comes running towards mill and disappears from sight inside.

(BAYING OF HOUNDS COMING NEARER)

M-86   INT. GROUND FLOOR OF MILL.

A small, circular room, just large enough to accommodate the pump-shaft and a rickety stairway leading up through a trap door opening in floor, to the top of the mill. Everything is in a state of decay. The pump-shaft is broken in several places - there are large holes in the floor, through which rank weeds are lifting their heads. A faint light is admitted through several places where the side walls of the mill have started to fall away. The only solid thing which remains is the door, of heavy oak, which is standing half open.

Monster burst in through the door, slamming it shut behind him, and dumping Frankenstein's body to the floor.

M-87   INT. MILL
       FLASH CLOSE SHOT DOOR

   matching action as it slams shut -
   a huge cross-bar drops down into
   place, dislodged by the violence
   of the slam.

M-88   EXT. HILLSIDE. FLASH CLOSE SHOT HOUNDS

   as they race by the camera up the
   hill towards the mill, in full cry.

M-89   EXT. FLASH WIDE ANGLE HILLSIDE

   shooting down - crowd of peasants
   headed by Baron and Victor are
   joined by the other group - they
   all swarm up the hill together
   into camera.

M-90   EXT. MOUNTAIN TRAIL

   A narrow trail winding around the
   side of a hill - steep cliffs
   leading to ravine below. A third
   party of searchers appear from
   around the bend of the trail - as
   they come into fore., torches held
   high above their heads, moving in
   single file, the leader points
   ahead with an excited exclamation

M-91   EXT. VERY L.S. MILL,

   as seen from viewpoint of new group.
   The first two parties - the Baron's
   and the other - comprising about a
   hundred men, all with flaming torches,
   are swarming like distant fireflies
   up towards the mill. The far-off
   baying of the hounds is faintly   (BAYING OF HOUNDS)
   but distinctly heard.

M-92   EXT. MOUNTAIN TRAIL

   The third party of searchers
   start off, pell-mell, in the direction of the mill.

M-93   EXT. MILL. WIDE ANGLE:

    Hounds break over the brow of the hill and dash across camera to the door of the mill, where they are brought up short by the closed door, snarling and snapping.

M-94   INT. MILL MED. SHOT

    Rickety stairs in fore., getting angle to include bolted door below. Monster has picked up Frankenstein and thrown him over his shoulder again - has climbed half-way up the rickety stairs, where he pauses briefly, glancing fearfully over his shoulder at sound of the hounds outside - then continues on up, through open trap-door leading to second floor level of mill.

(BAYING OF HOUNDS OUTSIDE MILL)

M-95   EXT. MILL. FLASH WIDE ANGLE

    as great crowd of peasants, with Baron and Victor in lead, rush up over the brow of the hill towards the mill.

M-96   INT. MILL
       MED. SHOT SECOND FLOOR LEVEL

    Monster has come up through the trap-door - kicks it shut after him and proceeds up a shaky wooden ladder to top floor of the mill, Frankenstein over his shoulder.

M-97   EXT. MILL. FLASH MED. CLOSE
       SHOT SIDE ANGLE AT DOOR

    as peasants swarm around lower part of mill - drag the dogs off - general confusion and shouting - torches bobbing wildly.

M-98   EXT. HILLSIDE FLASH WIDE ANGLE

    A fourth group of searchers are hurrying up the hill from another direction towards the mill - great excitement

M-99   INT. TOP FLOOR OF MILL

    This room is smaller than the ones below, in proportion to the tapering structure of the mill - also in better repair, although everything is thick with dust and festooned with cobwebs. In one corner are a couple of moldering sacks of grain, half-eaten by rats, and the rusty remains of some machine parts. A small door, sagging inward, leads out upon a narrow balcony which encircles the upper part of the mill. There is also a small window hear the door. Through door the sails occasionally dip into sight and up again, slowly turning in the night wind. The room is dimly lit by light from half-open door and window, as well as by oblique shafts of light which enter through holes in the roof.
Monster has dumped Frankenstein down upon the dust-covered floor and is crouched by the window, peering down at the mob.

M-100   EXT, MILL FLASH L.S.

    shooting down through window. A great gathering of peasants with their torches - yelling and shouting - the continual baying of hounds.

(SOUNDS FROM CROWD CONTINUOUS

M-101   INT. FLASH LARGE CU MONSTER

    shadowy against the window.

THROUGHOUT ENTIRE

M-102   INT. LARGE CU FRANKENSTEIN

    slowly coming to. His eyes flicker open - he lies without moving for a moment, staring blankly up at the ceiling - then becomes conscious of the disturbance outside - raises himself slowly and painfully on one elbow and looks across towards Monster -

SEQUENCE)

M-103   INT. FLASH CU MONSTER

    swaying back and forth, growling to himself - terrified - at bay.

M-104   INT. CLOSE SHOT FRANKENSTEIN.

Sight of the Monster and the yelling outside brings him back with a rush to a sharp realization of his peril, as well as fact that aid is near at hand - he glances swiftly about for some means of escape.

M-105   INT. FLASH CU DOOR

as seen by Frankenstein

M-106   INT. CLOSE SHOT FRANKENSTEIN

as he starts very cautiously to drag himself over to the door - CAMERA PANNING SLOWLY TO FOLLOW Half-way across the dim room, he knocks against one of the disused machine parts and utters a sharp gasp of pain.

M-107   INT. FLASH CU MONSTER,

whirling at the sound.

M-108   INT. FLASH CU FRANKENSTEIN,

seeing that he is discovered - starts slowly to rise to his feet, to make a dash for the door.

M-109   INT. LARGE CU MONSTER

coming into camera towards Frankenstein, his face a livid mask of fear and hate.

M-110   INT. FLASH CU FRANKENSTEIN

leaping to his feet and staggering back.

M-111   EXT. MILL MED. CLOSE SHOT AT DOOR

    Peasants trying to batter down the door, which is quivering under their savage onslaughts, but so far has resisted them.

> PEASANTS
>
> Get a big log! .. some rocks!
> ... smash it down! ...

M-112   INT. MILL. WIDE ANGLE

    Frankenstein and Monster maneuvering slowly, craftily - Monster trying to force Frankenstein into a corner - blacking doorway - Frankenstein - stalling for a chance to make his bolt for freedom. Finally succeeds in drawing the Monster away from his position by pretending to start down ladder to second floor - as Monster makes quick move to block this, Frankenstein rushes across room and out of the door - Monster leaps after him with a snarl of rage.

M-113   EXT. MILL MED. SHOT BALCONY

    matching action as Frankenstein rushes out - Monster close at his heels - makes a grab for him - they grapple. A shout goes up from below.

M-114   EXT. FLASH MED SHOT PEASANTS,

    shooting from slight elevation - all heads are turned aloft.

M-115   EXT. FLASH MED SHOT PEASANTS

    shooting up - the figures of Frankenstein and Monster are seen struggling furiously.

M-   M-116   EXT. FLASH CU VICTOR,

    crying in horror:

M-116 (CONTINUED)

                    VICTOR

                    Henry!

M-117   EXT. FLASH CU BARON

    looking up, startled

M-118   EXT. FLASH L.S. BALCONY,

    shooting up - one of the sails swings around, blotting the two figures from view of the crowd beneath. Roar of the crowd increases.

M-119   EXT. CLOSE SHOT ON BALCONY,

    as Monster hurls Frankenstein back in through the door - then turns and bares his teeth in an animal snarl at the peasants below - a yell goes up from the mob.

M-120   EXT. WIDE ANGLE,

    shooting down - all the peasants gazing aloft and yelling at the top of their voices.

                    PEASANTS

                    There he is! ... The
                    fiend! ... murderer! ...
                    kill him ... kill! ...
                    kill! ...

    The din becomes almost deafening.

M-121   EXT. FLASH LARGE CU MONSTER

    looking down and snarling -

M-122   EXT. MED. SHOT PEASANTS

    A couple of them reach down and snatch up rocks, hurling them aloft.

M-123   EXT. MED. SHOT ANOTHER GROUP,

following suit - hurling stones and yelling like maniacs -

M-124   EXT. FLASH CU MONSTER

as a stone grazes his temple - he recoils as a shower of stones fall around him, many of them reaching their mark.

M-125   EXT. MILL FLASH CU FRANKENSTEIN pulling himself up from the floor and staggering out of the door again.

M-126   EXT. HILL. FLASH WIDE ANGLE MOB,

yelling and hurling stones -

M-127   EXT. MED. SHOT BALCONY.

Frankenstein comes lurching out from inside, very weak - barely able to stand - slips behind the Monster's back, as if to run around to other side of balcony. Monster turns and lunges after him.

M-128   EXT. FLASH CLOSE SHOT BARON AND VICTOR

screaming up to Frankenstein:

> BARON AND VICTOR
>
> Jump, Henry! Jump!   Jump!

M-129   EXT. MED. SHOT BALCONY,

shooting from just a little below balcony level. Frankenstein, bewildered and dazed with pain and desperation, starts to obey - gets one leg over the balcony rail just as Monster grabs him and yanks him back.

M-130   EXT. FLASH CLOSE SHOT BARON

He jerks rifle to shoulder
and fires.

M-131   EXT. FLASH CLOSE SHOT MONSTER

as Baron's shot takes effect
catching him in the chest - he
screams with rage and pain -
swings Frankenstein around in
front of him, pinioning him by
the arms- another shower of
stones and clubs fall around him
and Frankenstein.

M-132   EXT. CLOSE SHOT LUDWIG

raising his rifle to fire again.

M-133   EXT. MED. CLOSE SHOT

as Baron springs into scene
dashing the rifle from Ludwig's
hands, crying.

                    BARON

               No - no! My son - !

Ludwig jerks himself loose
and again raises his rifle
snarling:

                    LUDWIG

               What about my little girl?

fires twice.

M-134   EXT. CLOSE SHOT BALCONY

Frankenstein cries out in pain
as he receives the two shots
square in the chest - sags forward.

M-135   EXT. FLASH LARGE CU BARON,

as he sees effect of shots - turns
upon Ludwig with a cry of agonized
fury,

M-136   EXT MED. SHOT

    Baron and Ludwig in immediate fore. - matching action as Baron swings around on Ludwig and fells him with one terrific blow. The peasants yell all the louder at this - they surge forward and sweep the struggling Baron back out of their way. Victor springs angrily to his assistance, but receives the same treatment - general melee - the mob has gone absolutely wild.

M-137   EXT. MED. CLOSE SHOT AT DOOR

    Some of the men have found a heavy log, which they are using as a battering-ram, but without much success. They are joined by another group with upraised torches, who rush in crying:

                    PEASANTS

                      Never mind that! Burn the mill . . . Burn the mill! . .

    this cry is taken up by others, out of scene.

M-138   EXT. WIDER ANGLE

    matching action as the cry becomes louder:

                    PEASANTS

                      Burn the mill! . . . Burn the mill! . . .

    They start rushing into camera screaming insanely.

M-139   EXT. MED SHOT ANOTHER ANGLE

    Baron vainly trying to struggle through the milling mob, calling desperately:

                    BARON

                    No, no! I forbid it! My son - my son - !

M-140   EXT. FLASH MED. CLOSE SHOT

as peasants crowd forward and start
piling their burning torches around
the base of the mill.

M-146   EXT. BALCONY FLASH LARGE
         CU MONSTER

shooting up from point
slightly below balcony level -
Monster looking down over rail -
his eyes light up with increasing
fear at what he sees.

M-147   EXT. L.S. SIDE OF MILL,

shooting down from balcony. Around
the base of the mil is a circle of
fire, formed by the heaped-up
torches. More and more peasants are
crowding forward, hurling their
torches upon the rapidly-mounting
pyre. The mill has already ignited
and flames have commenced to like
up the side.

M-148   EXT. FLASH MED. SHOT BASE OF MILL

A great pile of blazing torches in
immediate fore. - peasants moving
forward from b.g. in great numbers,
casting their torches into pile -
the flames shoot up, almost obliter-
ating men in b.g.

M-144   EXT. MED. SHOT BALCONY.

Monster recoils, chattering fearfully -
starts jumping up and down in a frenzy -
rushes to rail and yells down below,
making frantic gesticulations - then
looks around for something to furl down
at the peasants. Frankenstein has
slumped down in a heap on the narrow
balcony - Monster leaps at him and picks
him up to throw him over the rail.
Frankenstein struggles feebly - utters
a cry of despair

M-145   EXT., FLASH CU BARON

    glancing aloft - a cry of helpless horror bursts from his lips as he points -

M-146   EXT. FLASH L.S.

    shooting to top of mill, as Monster stands at balcony rail, with the struggling body of Frankenstein poised above his head -

M-147   EXT. FLASH CLOSE SHOT BALCONY

    as the Monster, with a mighty bellow hurls Frankenstein's body down at the mob.

M-148   EXT. FLASH L.S.

    shooting down - Frankenstein's body hurtling down towards upraised faces of the horrified peasants -

M-149   EXT. FLASH LARGE CU BARON,

    his face a mask of helpless agony

M-150   EXT. FLASH LARGE CU VICTOR

    crying out and averting his eyes.

M-151   EXT. SIDE OF MILL

    A large sheet of flame shoots up the side.

M-152   EXT. WIDE ANGLE.

    Peasants rushing by camera towards spot where Frankenstein's body has fallen

M-153   EXT. FLASH MED. L.S. MILL

at one of the sails, swinging slowly down towards flames, catches fire - continues on up, carrying fire with it.

M-154   EXT. MED. SHOT BALCONY

shooting at balcony level. Monster jumping up and down - the flaming sail passes by between him and the camera - he leaps back in stark terror.

M-155   EXT. MED. CLOSE SHOT

Baron in immediate fore., back to camera, kneeling over his son's lifeless body (out of scene) - his head bowed in grief. Victor stands beside him, one hand on his shoulder, also gazing down. Peasants exchange horrified glances - then start to withdraw, leaving the two men alone in their desolation.

M-156   EXT. FLASH MED. L.S. MILL

Another sail catches fire - the lower portion of the mill is now wrapped in flames.

M-157   EXT. BALCONY FLASH CU MONSTER

shrinking back as the fiery sails swing between him and camera.

M-158   EXT. FLASH MED. SHOT PEASANTS

watching the fire - CAMERA PANS SWIFTLY ALONG as they point and yell in triumph, the light of the holocaust on their sweaty animal faces.

M-159   EXT. FLASH WIDE ANGLE

    Another shot of the blazing structure. One of the great sails breaks loose and crashes to the ground in a shower of sparks and debris.

M-160   EXT. MED. SHOT AT BALCONY LEVEL,

    as the remaining sails swing around, a little faster, all of them blazing now, like a gigantic pin-wheel of flame.

M-161   EXT. FLASH LARGE CU MONSTER'S FACE

    as he screams with terror - smoke and flame enveloping him. We hear the ominous swish of the blazing wings - the loud crackle of flame.

M-162   INT. MILL.

    Monster rushes in from the outside up the center of the mill shoots a spurt of flame and smoke - Monster turns, trapped - rushes outside again, screaming.

M-163   EXT. MILL MED. SHOT BALCONY LEVEL

    The wings are turning faster - at intervals we see the figure of the Monster, leaping up and down yelling like a veritable fiend - the heavy rising pall of black smoke blots him out. CAMERA STARTS MOVING BACK as we

            DISSOLVE THROUGH TO

M-164   EXT. VERY L.S. MILL

    from adjoining hillside. On the crest of the hill the mill is a solid sheet of flame - the great sails turning and breaking up, another crashes down - the mob runs back out of the way - remain at about a hundred yards from the mill, watching and yelling.

                    FADE OUT

SEQUENCE "N"

(SOLEMN TOLLING
OF CHURCH BELL)

FADE IN TO

N-1   INT. VILLAGE CHURCH. DAWN.
      LARGE CU OF SINGLE CANDLE ON
      ALTAR, burning low. CAMERA
      MOVES BACK TO INCLUDE CU
      ELIZABETH, kneeling in front
      pew, her head bowed in silent
      prayer. She raises her head and   (SOUND OF DOOR
      looks around at the sound of a door   OPENING)
      opening behind her.

N-2   INT. L.S. CHURCH
      shooting towards entrance door,
      Elizabeth in immediate fore.
      The church is empty and in deep
      shadow. Lit only by candle - light
      and the first faint glimmer of
      the dawn. From b.g. comes the
      Baron and Victor, walking very
      slowly. The Baron looks old and
      haggard - every line of his drooping
      body spells defeat and despair.
      Victor is half-guiding, half-sup-
      porting him. Elizabeth's hand
      flies to her throat in a quick
      gesture of foreboding.   (CHURCH

                                              BELLS

N-3   INT. CU BARON AND VICTOR   TOLLING

      coming forward into camera, which   SLOWLY
      moves back before them The Baron's
      head is bowed - he seems oblivious   UNTIL
      to everything but his great sorrow.
      As they approach the front of the   FINAL
      church, CAMERA SWINGS AROUND TO
      WIDER ANGLE, taking in Elizabeth   FADE)
      She makes an involuntary move
      towards Victor and the Baron, her
      eyes agonized in silent pleading -
      Victor makes a swift gesture,
      indicating that she is not to speak.
      He releases his hold on the Baron's
      arm and turns to Elizabeth - the
      Baron moves on past them, unheeding -
      CAMERA PANS WITH HIM as he reaches
      chancel steps. Here he raises his
      eyes for a brief moment and then
      falls to his knees
      before the altar. CAMERA MOVES
      FORWARD TO CLOSE SHOT as he
      lies there, physically spent,
      emotionally exhausted, his clasped
      hands trembling as he lowers his
      head into his arms

N-4   INT. CLOSE SHOT VICTOR AND ELIZABETH

standing beside a pillar. Elizabeth's head is bowed, also. Victor has his arm consolingly about her shoulder - there are tears in his eyes, but he is otherwise in control of himself. As they stand there, the light of the dawn commences to steal in through a large stained-glass window over the chancel, slowly suffusing them with it's rays. CAMERA STARTS MOVING BACK TO L.S. CHURCH - the last thing we see is Victor and Elizabeth standing by the pillar and the morning sun breaking over them - while in b.g., kneeling before the shadowy altar, the broken figure of the old Baron. CAMERA MOVES BACK AT INCREASED TEMPO to the very doors of the church, which close slowly as CAMERA PASSES THROUGH and we

FADE OUT

Appendix A

June 11th, 1931

To. Dick Schayer   From   Mr. Henry Henigson

With regard to "FRANKENSTEIN":

1. My major objection is that there is no comedy relief whatever in the picture, and I think that this is extremely important at certain points and should be injected, ever if it is done thru incidental characters, to relieve the tension from time to time. I don't think the relief of the love affair is sufficient in as much as the present love affair is not a most satisfactory one, in the sense of the girl apparently being deeply in love with Henry and she takes Victor as a compromise.

2. I think that everyone in the picture should speak perfect English and we should take away the "Yahs, Herrs and Frau leins" and the twists in construction of the language which give it Teutonic distinction. We are not trying to place this picture geographically, in any particular spot, and I think that we can attempt to this by taking the Teutonic element out of it.

3. The script at the present time in considerably over-length. It takes long to say certain things. The following remarks are more or less detailed, but reactions which I got in reading the script:

Sequence B. Opens with an Interior. I am wondering, since the set is required later on in the picture especially the village I think the dissolves, that is at present provided for in A and B will be a little tough to take, even if the medium of the picture is used. This first sequence is very gruesome and I think a long fade would be better, coming into something lively in a long short of the village with the camera moving to the house. The abruptness is what bothers me here. This sequence attempts to get over the following story points: 1. That Henry is a Doctor. 2. That he is engaged to Elizabeth. 3. That Victor is a suitor and Henry's best friend. 4. Henry is involved in secret work. 5. That Victor decides to go.

In Sequence C. I would like to get a couple of the ideas over as outlined in GREENFIRE. I mean from a scientific point of view. Also, in Scene C - 9, where Waldron is describing where Henry is working, I wonder if it wouldn't be practical and possible to plant the geography, possibly thru the windows of University, of a place in the mountain fastnesses in the distance, so that the audience could visualize the fact, clarifying the geography.

Sequence D. This opens with a straight - on shot of the tower at night. I guess this is a matter of set construction, but if the construction permits it I would like to see a moving shot here, getting the camera into motion. In Scene 3, in the last line from Henry, I would like to lose the words "Those high frequency wires". I mean by this that "high frequency" is very commonly known today and I think that using these words make it too simple.

In D- 13 and 15, at three points on the rapping of Waldron rain effect should be provided for. I daresay the director would have this in mind.

In D - around 31. I think we ought to go into possibly calling attention to the cosmic ray definitely and take it into the realm of the most advance form of scientific discussion. In general, in sequence D, I think we can kill off considerable footage of the explanation, first thru the medium of the dwarf, and secondly, thru Waldron and Victor. I think we can establish the entrance of

Victor and Waldron faster and get into the story of the monster.

In Sequence E. This involves a series of lap-dissolves. I would like to see this killed off, into a travel shot so that as many scenes will not be required to get it over. It is better technique.

Sequence F. This starts in the village, carrying the burgomeister along the street in preparation for the wedding, and we then get a supplication of this when he enters the house, by establishing the village in the B sequence as previously stated; I think we can go direct to the interior and save this street walk. The entire sequence can stand considerable cutting. It is talkie stuff on an interior in the picture. There are just a couple of points to get over, which should be gotten over fast, incidental to the major part of the story, and in addition should be considerably broken up. It now runs seven pages on one scene number. This remark is made purely from a technical point of view in production, as regards company progress.

Sequence G - 5, contains lines that I think can be improved, according to the thoughts contained in GREENFIRE. I am wondering whether Sequence H is necessary. I would like very much to kill of the second scene, located in the lake, purely from a production point of view. There is no other lake business and we will have to leave the studio for this particular scene, which is described at WIDE ANGLE SUNSET. I am wondering whether this sequence can't go entirely.

Sequence I. Scene 3. Altho this is an insert, I think it should be provided for a simpler language - more staccato style.

Sequence J. Is a long sequence built for the purpose of getting the monster out on his first of a series of ravages. I am wondering whether this entire sequence cannot be eliminated and in an Impressionistic way, thru a series of Dissolves, and get over everything we want to instead of starting to build up family sympathy at this point of the story; it is this part of the story that we will eventually bring the monster in to do the killing, when we do it the next time.

I think it is all right in Sequence K, because we are actually building up to a point of where this man becomes an important part of our story. I am speaking of the father of the girl.

L - 29. I would like the word "slain" to be changed to "killed or murdered". I don't think that a trapper would use the word "slain".

In Sequence M. - where the crowd starts out to get to the Monster. I think we ought to move this faster in getting to him, by eliminating footage. It is expensive material to shoot, as now written, and your suspense actually comes from the moment that the Monster is "spotted", and I think in cutting the picture we will find that that is a point we will have to get to quickly.

All in all, I consider the script an exceptionally good one and with some comedy relief, has every good quality.

Appendix B

JUNE 13, 1931

TO
MR SCHAYER

FROM
GARRETT FORT

SUBJECT:

REACTIONS TO MR. HENIGSON'S REACTIONS TO "FRANKENSTEIN"

1. No comedy relief.

    There is undoubtedly some need for comedy relief, but owing to the character of the story and the length of the script in its present form. I see no way to inject this beyond utilizing minor characters in whatever sequences such comedy can be used without appearing dragged in. Certainly we have no room for the introduction of any more characters for comedy purposes nor for the footage it would require to build these characters into a spot where they could be legitimately acceptable as such.

    Relief of love affair sufficient, etc.
    Girl is not deeply in love with Henry, and she does love Victor. As brought out in dialogue, her wedding to Henry is the result of a childhood arrangement between families, quite in keeping with the Continental conception of such matters. She is fond of Henry - admires him - is sympathetic and fascinated by him - her emotions when she finds him in trouble are not those of love, but pity. She has voluntarily given up Victor because of obligations she feels she cannot sidestep and Henry's death provides a happy culmination of a repressed romance which certainly would seem to be satisfactory all around. Henry is an abnormal character - the Victor and girl characters are normal people. The audience will therefore be rooting for them, although at the same time sympathetic towards Henry because of his ill-starred love, wreaked because of his absorption in science. The girl in her scenes with Henry will receive all the sympathy in the world, because we realize that she is making the best of a bad bargain, but doing it like a thoroughbred, never giving Henry the slightest inkling of her real feelings.

2. Teutonic objections

    In a story laid in and around Goldstadt, with names like Frankenstein, Waldman, Moritz, Goldstadt, Fritz, etc. it seems that a Teutonic slant is inescapable. If we intend to lay it elsewhere it will be necessary to change every name in the cast, probably even that of Frankenstein, which certainly has Teutonic connotations. This might lead to titles such as "The Monster," "Garabaldi," or "Love and Murder in Norway," etc. I have an idea that there is nothing offensive about the Teutonic slant, as nobody shows any signs of being more than an ordinary type of bastard - in fact, they all derive a certain sympathy - and it is a particularly pertinent angle when we consider that the Teutonic type of mind is certainly the foremost in the scientific world, etc.

3. Length of script

Certainly can be cut down, but I feel this is a matter which should be fully discussed with the director. Until a director is definitely asigned, it seems alot of waste motion to go over ground that may have to be gone all over again with a possible resultant confusion and loss of certain values of temp, mood etc.

Sequence B:

No value in showing a long shot of village, as nothing happens in such a shot that contributes anything to movement of picture, and would be static and probably cut out later. We are not so much concerned with the geography of this sequence as we are with its emotional content - i.e., that here is Frankenstein's fiancee and that she's worried and that she loves Victor, etc. The quiet setting and feeling between the two unhappy lovers affords a direct and interesting contrast to the scenes of horror that have just gone before. The less we show of the village in this sequence, the less chance we run of confusing an audience. The mere fact that we omit village intensifies the feeling that we want to get - that Frankenstein is far away. Otherwise the audience might subconsciously wonder why the hell the girl doesn't go see Frankenstein herself - if the peasants we saw in the funeral procession didn't come from that village - etc. The remoteness of Frankenstein from the chalet is made subconsciously clearer by not definitely establishing his contact with the chalet or the chalet's relation to the village. There will be nothing abrupt about the Dissolve from F's CU at the gibbet into the CU of his picture - in face, the sharp contrast serves as an aid to dramatic speed.

Sequence C

    While "Green Fire" may be a swell play and contain many interesting lines, the subject matter of our story is so radically different that I feel we will only achieve a synthetic result which will not in any way clarify, dignify, or enhance what is already in the script, and may only serve to confuse. My experience in trying to fit together unrelated lines and scenes has shown me that it is rarely successful, and serves no purpose. If a story is clear and right, there should be no need for useless verbal or dramatic appendages. If the story isn't right, then it's the dramatist's fault and he should be obliged to clarify matters by the employment of his own resources rather than crib from somebody else. Otherwise, he's taking money under false pretences and should be led gently but firmly to the front gate and given the air.

    C-9. It will be both practical and swell to follow out Mr. Henigson's idea of suggesting locale by back-drops. This can be done very nicely in scenes on top of tower, where dwarf in fooling around with the wires. As he indicates it is entirely a matter of set construction. There is an open door in upper tower room, but there must be no big windows. Frankenstein's whole idea of fixing up a place like that is for the purpose of privacy and he certainly wouldn't pick out a spot with a flock of windows to conduct secret researches.

Sequence D

    Objections to straight-on shot of tower. This might be made a most effective bit of pictorial composition. However, it is completely immaterial about the straight-on shot, and I think Mr. Henigson's idea about a moving shot would be swell, especially if we use a miniature for the set -up.

    Technical language about "high-frequencey wires", etc., should be checked with electrical department. I went to considerable trouble to do just this, and found that in their opinion, it is better to have terms that mean something to technical men in audience than to manufacture some phoney terms that would only get a snicker from those in the know. In these days when every kid in the audience has his own radio and the old folks talk about superheterodynes and television, there isn't much chance of getting away with it

D-13 - 15.
Rain will be provided.

D-31
Calling attention to cosmic ray and taking it "into the realm of the most advanced form of scientific discussion," etc. This realm is a little beyond my mental grasp and I will have to regretfully refer it to someone who is more at home with his cosmic affinities. Don't you think that the less actual scientific palaver we have, the more convincing it will be? Long, pseudo-scientific discussions in a scene like this might only serve to retard the action even more that it is, and if, as Mr. Henigson indicates, this sequence needs cutting. I don't think it would help much to put in a lot of dialogue which would be completely unintelligible to the majority of audiences - and probably silly to the initiated.

No explanations can be killed off through the medium of the dwarf, who is dumb. If we make him articulate, it only means writing in dialogue for him all through the script, which will defeat our purposes in attempting to achieve brevity.

Entire sequence can undoubtedly be cut down, especially entrance and exits, but it much be made slow enough to be impressive, as it is the key sequence of our story. In other words, if the audience isn't completely impressed by the elaborate build-up for the creation of the Monster, they won't be impressed by anything that follows:

Sequence E.
Mr. Henigson has misunderstood purpose of dissolves. Action does not take place along village street, but in three distinctly different locales. The point we tried to make in these three shots was that the entire surrounding countryside had become aware that all was not well in the lonely tower on the hill - not just merely one little village

Sequence F:

    Sequence can start in interior if necessary. My only thought on the moving exterior shot was to show the village for color, relief from the grimness of preceding sequence, and now that comedy element seems necessary to give us a chance for some. If we do not establish the great interest the village has in the wedding and the importance of Frankenstein's status there, it might seem a bit incongruous later on to find the same village in such elaborate festal array. While the burgomeister gets over the interest just as well in his dialogue in the house, it still remains true that it is always better to show something than to talk about it.

    All dialogue in house in important, and should not be trimmed too much. The love scene is the only other one between Victor and Elizabeth in the picture and seems necessary to foreshadow our ending, where they eventually get together.

    In final shooting script, this sequence will be broken up into ten or fifteen scene numbers, as requested for the good of company progress.

Sequence G-5

    Previous remarks about "Green Fire" apply equally here.

    Sequence H absolutely necessary for relief and preparation for wedding sequence.

    As far as lake shot is concerned, this is O. K. with me. Can be laid in garden. However, Mr. Florey has some ideas about this and I would suggest he be given a chance to express himself before we slash.

Sequence I:

> O.K. on simpler insert, although let's not lose the medical feeling.

Sequence J:

> Can be cut down to possible five or six impressionistic shots. Is not really as long as it looks, the writing in of detail making it seem so. Florey has definite ideas about shooting this with considerable effectiveness and I'd Suggest checking with him in this case, also... We are not attempting to build up "family sympathy", merely showing the type of people menaced by such a Monster and also to show a nice, light little scene of family life to point up the horror of such and unexpected horror stalking abroad - I feel sequence is not only sound but damned interesting dramatically and will be O.K. when cut down a little.

L-29

> "Slain" happens to be a word of effective simplicity entirely in keeping with the man with says it. Remember the vocabulary of these mountain-folk is limited and that a feeling of simplicity is quite in keeping with the character. We used "Killed" and "murdered" for other characters - this word is introduced for a definite purpose.

Sequence M:

> Whole sequence will be snapped up and cut down. Most shots are three-foot flashes - some only 12 frames, as indicated. Sequence is one that will probably be shot according to requirements of director and Limitations of location, so there isn't much we can do until we get down to actual productions and schedule.
>
> IN GENERAL, feel there is nothing in the way of actual re-writing to be done, and most changes depend upon who will direct. As soon as this is definitely set, we can go over script and touch it up here and there, but at this point it is accordingly vague. Will be perfectly willing to help in any way I can when production is set and plans are under way.

G.E.F.

Appendix C

BRIEF SYNOPSIS OF "FRANKENSTEIN"

by

GARRETT FORT

On a remote mountain-top not far from a small university town in Central Europe, young Henry Frankenstein, scholar and fanatic, has converted an old windmill into a laboratory, where he is engaged in the secret task of creating a human being

Born in the midst of a fierce electrical storm, amidst weird surroundings, Frankenstein's creature emerges as a huge hulk of a man, a monster of terrific strength, feeble intelligence, and a vast potentiality for evil.

Despite the pleas of his friends, his family and his sweetheart, Frankenstein endeavors to raise his creature to a level of human intelligence, but only succeeds in arousing the worst side of the monster, who escapes and spreads murder and havoc through the countryside. In very short order, the whole region is stricken with terror as the monster rages, unchecked, leaving death and desolation in his wake.

Brought to a sharp realizatons of the enormity of his crime against his fellow-men, Frankenstein tries to undo his wrong, to destroy his creation. Meanwhile, the monster has innocently killed a little child, the daughter of a weedcutter, a girl of ten who has approached him without fear and in whose presence his wild savagery is momentarily stilled.

The peasants throughout the countryside rise in revolt against this final outrage, and in a great manhunt, with torches, dogs, and weapons, band together to track down the monster. He takes refuge in the mill, the one place he regards as sanctuary, and there he comes face to face with the man who has so wrongfully given him life, so thoughtlessly brought him into a modern world with only half-formed animal instincts to guide him.

Tracked down by a raging mob, both Frankenstein and his monster perish dramatically as the mill is fired by the furious peasants.

Throughout the story runs a love theme of beauty and tenderness - that of a lovely young girl and Frankenstein's best friend, denying themselves because of their attachment for their companion, and who are happily united at his spectacular death.

www.ingramcontent.com/pod-product-compliance
Lightning Source LLC
Chambersburg PA
CBHW082039230426
43670CB00016B/2709